The She

Manage like a Shepherd

An Ancient Principle That Builds Strong Leaders
and Stable Companies That Grow

Mark E. Peters

ISBN 978-1-0980-8350-2 (paperback)
ISBN 978-1-0980-8351-9 (digital)

Christian Faith Publishing, Inc.
832 Park Avenue
Meadville, PA 16335
www.christianfaithpublishing.com

Printed in the United States of America

CONTENTS

THE SHEPHERD THEORY

Manage like a Shepherd

Have you ever had a star employee come into your office and give you their resignation or have troubles keeping great employees? Do you have difficulties finding quality individuals to hire? Is your company growing or shrinking? Maybe there is something going on that you may not be aware of. I have always managed my companies using an ancient principle. Yes, it is biblical, but it is a great model for managing a company. If you are suffering growth, having a high employee turnover, and want to correct this trend, read on if you dare!

A psalm of David:

> The Lord is my shepherd; I shall not be in want.
> He makes me lie down in green pastures;
> he leads me beside quiet waters,
> he restores my soul.
> He guides me in paths of righteousness
> for his name's sake.
> Even though I walk
> through the valley of the shadow of death,
> I will fear no evil,
> for you are with me;
> your rod and your staff,
> they comfort me.
> You prepare a table before me

in the presence of my enemies.
You anoint my head with oil;
my cup overflows.
Surely goodness and love will follow me
all the days of my life,
and I will dwell in the house of the Lord
forever. (Psalm 23)

This is probably the most read verse from the Bible. It is usually read to define the protection granted from the Lord. It also sets the foundation for the definition of a *shepherd*. We will use this as the road map to the success of shepherding. It also is interesting to know that the word *shepherd* is used over one hundred times in the Bible and is always used to define a caretaker. We are about to explore why the shepherd theory works today and sets the rules for a successful manager and company.

We will look at this later on as a management style to which we can try to achieve. I agree this would be pretty tough to follow, but it is the ultimate shepherd. Jesus was referred to as the great shepherd. He sets an example for us on how to be a good shepherd.

ACKNOWLEDGMENTS

Special thanks to the following:

Pastor Dave Hastings
Eastside Christian Church
Pastor Dave reviewed my biblical content and is a great spiritual lead pastor.

Pastor Charles McCaskey
First Cumberland Presbyterian Church
He reintroduced Christ to me and ordained me as an elder.

My wife, Debora, my son, Chad, and daughter, Liane
My family supported me throughout my career and put up with all the moves. This included a total of six major moves and four local moves.

I would also like to thank the following pastors:

Brian Law
Jeff Raker
Wendy McCormick
These pastors were not only great spiritual leaders but now are good friends and have always been there for our family.

In loving memory of my parents
Irving and Mildred who gave me the freedom to chase my dreams

My friend and business partner, Giovanni Soldo
Giovanni and I worked together as business partners for more than twenty years. Together we built two successful businesses with the help of great employees.

INTRODUCTION

What Is a Company?

Some define their company by the products they produce. Others define it by names and logos. Still others define it by service, quality, or ISO or Six Sigma quality programs. Companies grow because of successful products and services, but most forget how they got there. Where did the products come from? Who is responsible for quality? Does it just happen? Is it built in to the company? Of course not, quality is people. If you have success through quality, it is good leadership and people who care. If you have bad quality, then there is a lacking in leadership direction and people that do not understand the requirements for quality. Why does a company exist? Some say it is to make money and produce profits while keeping investors and directors satisfied. When a company loses focus on the people, the product, and the customer and puts profits and systems ahead of these, they are going to fail. Good people will leave. Then customers will leave, and then the company downsizes and eventually fails.

Let's look at today's system. What caused the US car companies to fail? I think they lost focus on the customer needs and the employee's satisfaction. They need unions to manage the employee because the company can't manage them correctly or fairly. Unions are required when companies don't take care of the flock. I think unions should be a thing of the past; but if you are not taking care of your people, they will get a union to help them with this. If you treat your employees as your most important asset, there would be no unions.

Why do companies fail? Is it changes in the economy or changes in the marketplace? These are all great excuses; but in reality, it is "shepherd failure" companies change. With good leadership and with good and satisfied people, they evolve, survive, and grow.

IBM, for example, do they still make typewriters? Kodak is changing from a film company to a digital company; Apple has reinvented itself many times. I can't wait to see what the refineries are going to do when we change the way we fuel the transportation of the world. This will be very interesting. We use a lot of oil-based products from plastics to waxes to lubricants. Also, when you look around at the amount of plastic, there still is a huge demand of oil-based product. Anyway, the companies that will survive will evolve. This will only happen with the right leadership and people.

Failure, we have seen a lot of this in the last fifteen years. What was the cause? Mostly greed, but loss of communication with the employees and the customer is a fallout of this greed, not understanding the product and worshipping the dollar, executives that are self-centered and very greedy.

> For the love of money is the root of all kinds of evil. And some people, craving money, have wandered from the true faith and pierced themselves with many sorrows. (1 Timothy 6:10)

This scripture really gets confusing for some; it is not saying that money is evil, but what it is saying the *love* of money can be the cause of evil. When money becomes the main focus in the company, decisions are made on money issues and not how it will affect employees, customers, and even the respect you would or will get in your industry. Many sorrows can refer to the failures in a company and the loss of customers and good, hardworking, and loyal employees.

Let's examine a few companies that failed (many sorrows) because the shepherds did not follow the rule of making the sheep the most important part of the business.

Enron basically failed because of greed, looking out for themselves and not the customer or the employee. I can name a few, but it was discovered that executives were inflating the stock price through numerous techniques and misleading public information. They described technological achievements of Enron that did not occur. They boasted about the value and financial performance of the company even when it was on the verge of failure. Executives described a network superior to their competitors, even though it was not. All of this was created to inflate the stock price and thus the money they would earn. All of this was being done as executives traded Enron securities inside the company while they had nonpublic information about the business, aka insider trading. Five executives alone were found to have made a total of $150 million off of these schemes.

Banks failed due to bad loans, basically too risky and were destined to fail. Why did this occur? Greed, selling loans is a major part of the banking business; and the more you sell, the more you make, unless the person borrowing the money defaults on the loan. This came from too many risky options offered from the bank to attract borrowers, but it was also a fault or lack of understanding from the consumer what they really were getting into. The consumer looked at the immediate future and did not consider where the money would come from, when the interest rate inflated or kicked in, depending on the loan option. Then they ended up with a loan payment that was not going to fit into the budget. Then comes default and the make forecloses.

GM's failure after 101 years is a condemnation of American management in general. It exemplifies the damage to our economy when finance becomes the tail that wags the economic dog. It also shows what happens to any company that rests on its success and fails to adapt to change and lets the wolf (unions) manage the sheep.

They are dogs with mighty appetites; they never have enough. They are shepherds who lack understanding; they all turn to their own way, each seeks his own gain. (Isaiah 56:11)

This was written over three thousand years ago, but I guess bad habits are hard to break; this scripture describes the typical failure of a company. Bad shepherds equal company failure. Usually self-centered greed tops the list; a true shepherd would always make decision in the best interest of the flock.

You probably won't believe this, but this is the truth! The most important asset in any company is the people, the sheep. When you lose this understanding, you will lose your company. Take away the people (sheep), what is left? People are the foundation of the company. The more you nurture your flock, the better your company will perform; it is the engine of the company. The better you take care of them, the better they will take care of the company.

CHAPTER 1

What Is a Shepherd?

Let's see what the Bible has to say about what a shepherd is.

> Be shepherds of God's flock that is under
> your care, serving as overseers—not because you
> must, but because you are willing, as God wants
> you to be; not greedy for money, but eager to
> serve. (1 Peter 5:2)

Ah, a servant! How many managers consider himself or herself as a servant? The most successful managers do. I don't care if it is employees or customers; the manager, just like our Great Shepherd, is a servant. You provide the care, benefits, and training for your flock. In turn, you will receive loyalty and quality work. In reality, you are building relationships. This is critical to keep customers and employees. If you do not serve your people, why in the world would they bother to provide any service for you? As a member of God's kingdom, a manager has a great responsibility. You are commissioned to serve, and do it focused on the people, not *money*, sounds crazy? No, let me explain. When you focus on money, you lose focus on the people. They lose focus on the goal, and you will lose money. Take care of the people; and they will take care of you, and you will be profitable. Money is the result of a well-structured company with leadership that serves its people; and the people, in turn, serve the company.

A great example of this outside the secular world is the modern church. Let's look at the megachurches. Are their goals, objectives, and focus on money? No! They are totally focus on people. After all, they do not have a "product" to sell, do they? They provide comfort, a safe place to worship and a place to learn and volunteer. There is no pressure on dress, and they serve warm drinks in the winter and cool drinks in the summer (coffee too).

Let's look at the department store and malls. What is taking them out? The Internet! Some stores are adapting to this and challenging the Internet, like a good example is the TJ Maxx group. They offer designer-based personal products at really discounted prices. Others are trying to figure this out and have been downsizing in non-performance areas, like JCPenney, Macy's and Kohl's. Others have closed, such as Toys R Us.

Best Buy is a place where you can see and hear tech products before you purchase; but the fear was they come, they look, and then they buy on the Internet. The solution shows the Internet price to the sales associate. And they will match it, and you leave that day with the product. This is a great example of listening to the client!

Some stores give you store cash based on what you spend. This really has helped store front sales; but yes, the Internet stores are catching up to this. Who will win, storefronts or the Internet? In a perfect world, they both could coexist. But will they? We will have to find out. My bet is the ones that best satisfy the customer needs, and there is no reason why both can survive if it is done right. Today some stores are becoming hubs for major online stores such as Amazon. This is a great step in the right direction both working together!

Understand what a shepherd is.

> Then Micah answered, "I saw all Israel scattered on the hills like sheep without a shepherd, and the Lord said, 'these people have no master. Let each one go home in peace.'" (2 Chronicles 18:16)

What are the traits of a good shepherd?

> He tends his flock like a shepherd: He gath-
> ers the lambs in his arms and carries them close
> to his heart. (Isaiah 40:11)

Do managers hold their employees close to their heart? If they want to be successful, they do. Do you run a company to satisfy your needs, or do you consider the employees first? Do you offer different benefits for management than the employees? If you want the best employees, you have to offer the best work environment. The better you treat an employee, the better they will treat you. Do you know your employees? Pick a time of day and visit the flock. Let them know you are there for them, answer questions, offer help, and let them know you are there for them.

I make sure I talk with or visit each employee every day. It is amazing to witness when I don't. They will ask me if everything is okay. How many of your employees would ask or care about your personal situation? They will if you care about them. It is okay to be close to your flock, of course. They are your most important assets. You should let your guard down; if you are guarded, they will be as well. Think about it; you spend from eight to ten hours a day with your work family. If you can't enjoy the people you work with, you have not done your job well! You are the leader, the coach, the mentor, and the visionary. You pick and lead the team who is going to make for the foundation of the company; this is what is going to hold it up.

Employees are people, and they come with human traits, sorrow, happiness, guilt, sadness, curiosity, pride, and most of all, feelings. Every decision you make affects all employees. Try not to surprise them as the results can be devastating. I have seen companies being sold and a huge setback because employees left, not understanding the reason behind the sale. Did it make sense for the sale? Probably so, but the employees did not understand the reason of the sale, and the trust barrier was destroyed. People left the company to find security.

Here is my life example: I worked in the corporate world for over twenty years. I moved many times to increase my experience and help the company where I thought my talents were needed. This company was a shepherd-style management company. I was impressed with all of my leaders and was even humbled in their presence. I watched and participated in many years of growth and also helped in times of recession, and we saw a few of those. My last tenure with this company was to operate a small part of the business, about forty employees in all. My boss, who ran about a 120-employee operation, and I operated the other part of the company. We were the specialized equipment—manufacturing division of a larger corporation that was expanding and growing through acquisitions and mergers. As a manager, I was given free rains to grow and produce products, expand markets, and hire when justified. I had a great shepherd; and to this day, he has been very successful. And after tenure as an entrepreneur, he sold his business with his employees' full involvement and is now an executive VP with the company that bought his company.

Anyway, I will call my boss Joe. Joe and I saw major changes in the management in the company, and we both now had a new report structure. Rumors of mergers were floating around. My new boss (I will call The Wolf) was meeting with me and telling me how I was going to operate from now on. This included changing report structures and marketing strategies. The Wolf was concentrating on money, not people, not talent, not emotions, but money. The Wolf was out to make a name for himself and all by himself. You were onboard this train, or you were left at the station, his words exactly. We went through all kinds of attitude, personality, and IQ testing. Rumors were flying everywhere, and nobody knew what was going on. The Wolf had created chaos, discomfort, and a scatter of the sheep. Joe and I both were looking at ways to leave this mess. It was out of our control, and we both agreed it was time to get off this train and find a new station. Joe went on to buy a small company and create a dream come true for him and his employees. I left and went to a smaller family-owned company and was a VP in charge of engineering.

Before Joe and I left, we met with our flocks and told them what we were doing, I feared for them, but I offered words of encouragement. And this was a very tear-shedding session. This is when I realized I was a true shepherd, and the love between the sheep and I was overwhelming. I felt bad for them, and I would have taken them all with me if I could have.

After I left, The Wolf and the pack decided they were going to build a new facility and move to an industrial complex not far away. Planning took place. Excitement grew, and about one month prior to moving, The Wolf dropped the bomb. "We are not moving. We are consolidating and reorganizing. You will be talked to about the plans. Some will be offered jobs, and others will be given packages as long as you stay through the shutdown and move."

Products were moving to the west and assembly to the south. Initially 20 were offered jobs out of 120. Most refused, and then they went to the B list, then the C list. In all, about 5 people accepted positions to move out of the 120 people. They would have to rebuild the company from the ground up. To make this story short, The Wolf was off to Mexico on a new assignment, and the split company with 5 employees divided between two locations was all that was left. What happened? People found new jobs. Some came with me on my entrepreneurial adventure; and believe it or not, more than 7 other entrepreneurs spawned out of this move. The bad news, a small pack of wolves basically destroyed a fast-growing product producing division of a large company on the theory of consolidation and integration would save lots of money. See, here is the issue: focus on money and not the employees or the clients affect the end result, losing 115 talented people, the advancement of product improvement and design. Did they recover? Well, The Wolf was ultimately discharged, and the company eventually got the products back up to par (and this took years to correct). The good news, the people prevailed and moved on to new ventures and jobs.

And David shepherded them with integrity of heart; with skillful hands he led them. (Psalm 78:72)

Leadership! That is what you need to provide. Do you provide the leadership needed to make the company successful? Do your employees know the goal of the company? Do they know when the company is thieving or suffering? They need to! I can't express this enough; you have to keep the people informed.

Life Experience

I moved to a smaller family-owned business with a young man in charge (owner's son) at that time, about twenty-eight years old. I was hired as the VP of engineering. I was brought into a group of engineers that I would consider similar to the *Island of Misfit Toys*. This group had no direction, leadership, or goals.

First thing I did was interview each employee reporting to me. I told them that I was there as a friend, and I was going to be an open book. They would be informed on company goals, direction, and objectives. I had to gain their confidence before I could get their respect. This was going to take time. They trusted no one. After the interviews, I laid out a chart with each of the people and what talents they brought to the department. My goal was first team, then organization, then our mission. All would be involved with the development of the mission and goals.

As I learned the talents, I developed sub groups or departments based on the talents of each of the individuals. I basically broke the engineering group into three departments: research and development, product support, and production engineering. Through a nonintrusive interview and strategic questions, I was able to ease tension, find out what they wanted to do and where the talent lied to fit properly with each department. The last thing you want to do is to put someone in a position that they do not want to be in or has no interest for them. After this, we had a party; and we got to know each other, along with spouses as well. We all became great friends.

During my tenure with this company, we developed eight new products along with multiple patents, and the company was growing at nearly 20 percent per year. This was done in less than a three-year period. I will say that I had pretty much free range, and the young president was a great marketer, but he lacked substantially in management skills (shepherding). But he was only twenty-eight, and he had a lot to learn. And I believed he had the potential to develop these skills. After I spent three years with this company, I decided to move in the direction of entrepreneur. I announced to the company and the engineering group that I was leaving to start my own business. The company had a luncheon for me, and I thanked them all and gave my condolences to the owners; and to my surprise, my group put together a going-away party for me. They put this together and not by the company. It was a happy and sad evening, but what I found was that I was doing something right. They did this for me, and that hit home for sure. I realized that it is important to treat how you would want to be treated.

I kept in touch with those I worked with; and not long after I left, the company went through many changes. And most of the engineers moved on, also about 25 percent of the rest of the company. Finally, after a few more years, the family sold the business to a large well-known company. Today the original owner got it. He is studying as a missionary and will enter a field of shepherding for the Lord.

As for me, I partnered with a business associate from the first company, and we went on to launch a successful manufacturing business that we grew to a fifty-plus-employee business over the next fifteen years. I absolutely attribute the growth and prosperity to following the principles within this theory. We had very little turnover and maintained steady growth. We invested money in growth and in employees. In fifteen years, we only took three disbursements. It was much wiser to invest in the growth of the company and our employees.

CHAPTER 2

The Shepherd Theory

> Shepherd your people with your staff, the
> flock of your inheritance, which lives by itself in
> a forest, in fertile pasturelands. Let them feed in
> Bashan and Gilead as in days long ago. (Micah
> 7:14)

This passage hits home for me. What it says: feed the flock with the best and provide a comfortable place to work. Use your staff to provide direction. Your staff is the most important tool and gets even more important as you grow. I can't say this enough. The better you care, the better they care! If you want your employees to perform their best, they must be provided with the best tools and the best equipment to best utilize and grow their skills. Feed them. It is okay to provide a lunch once in a while, have a chat, find out what's working and what isn't. You won't believe what can come out of a gathering of such. The information exchanged and new ideas produce usually far-out weigh the cost of the lunch. When it is time for a review make the employee feel special, take them to lunch. Celebrate the year and talk about business and, on a personal note, share with each other, get to know each other better.

Rules to Manage By

*I am the good shepherd. The good shepherd
lays down his life for the sheep. (John 10:11)*

How do I learn this theory?

How many managers define their own failure by blaming it on an employee or even multiple employees? Sometimes clients are dragged into the blame. A good board should see right through this. The shepherd protects his sheep. If the sheep are not performing, whose fault is this? I know it is impossible to be the perfect manager, but it is not impossible to be a successful manager. Sacrifice managers are the model sanctifiers. I have always lived by the rule to hire people like me or even smarter than me. I am not perfect by any means; but I think if you hire people with the same ideals as you, you will have a better team. It is also important to have personalities reflect and complement each other. What I'm saying is that even though they complement each other but, in the same way, they are completely opposite, this stimulates ideas, and ideas stimulates happy clients, and happy clients stimulate growth.

How do you spell shepherd?

S—Share. You need to do this. When you share the health of the company, there are no surprises. Also I have found when things are down, people get more creative. Let's face it. No one wants to lose his or her job. Also sharing knowledge makes everyone smarter. If you share your knowledge, you help people grow; and in turn, they help the company grow.

H—Help. You are there to support and supply resources. Remember a well-informed and well-trained employee makes a company stronger and more effective. You need to emphasize that anyone can ask for help and also anyone can provide help.

E—Equality. Every job is important. I don't care which one you pick. Everyone has talents, and you need to utilize them. Let's look at the receptionist, always an entry-level position in most companies, but this is the first voice a client hears on the phone and the first face a visitor sees when they enter the company. So how important is this? Look, the point is from reception to CEO, every job is important for company's success, and everyone should be treated as such!

P—Plan. A well-guided company has a well-planned path. This includes inside and out. What I mean is that the plan must include organizational to marketing planning. The plan must be agreed upon, have input from all and ownership. This makes a plan success-ful. Remember, share the plan with everyone, even customers. (Oh, did I say share again?)

H—Honesty. This is important. Remember, it is easier to tell the truth. You only have to remember one thing. Honesty keeps a company clean. What I am saying is that people make mistakes. Encourage honesty because in the end, lying hurts the company, but most of all, the client. Let me ask. Can you tell which companies you can trust and which ones you can't?

E—Empathy. If you don't have it, you need to learn it. This one is tough for almost everyone; but it is the ability to feel someone's pain and agony, putting you into their shoes. Listen and then respond. Do not interrupt. After they have finished, work with them through the problem. Work together for a solution. Don't try and solve it. Let them work it out with your guidance. They will then own it.

R—Resolve. Remember, you are a servant leader. You must be part of the solution. Too many times I have seen managers say "fix it your-self." When the manager leaves, I think there will be some negative contacts. When a client or an employee comes for help, they want you to be part of the solution.

D—Direct (the staff). This is the offering of guidance. Your job is to keep the focus on the plan, making sure everyone knows what it is and is participating to make it happen. This talent is a combination of all above. Leave one out and you will not be able to direct successfully.

Shepherds can have a flock of one to millions, of course, most are numbers under one hundred; but there are a few out there that tend to thousands, if not millions, (presidents of countries and, of course, large corporations). But one thing to remember is no matter what size your flock is, this is what your focus is "take care of the sheep, and they will take care of you."

Tasks:

1) To be a good shepherd, it is important that information is always available. Keep your door open. If you close it for any reason, let people know why; or if it is private, tell them it is private.
2) Never take someone from the opposite sex into a room without someone else or leave the door cracked open if it is to be more private.
3) Never make a promise you cannot keep.
4) Post company performance in an area for employees only. Keep this up to date on a monthly basis. This can include sale, shipments, on-time delivery, quality, and general information about what is going on.
5) If a client sends a letter about performance or quality of the company (good or bad), share it with the company.
6) Monthly brown-bag lunch event with all employees, make it required, and you will give a state of the company. And have a question-and-answer time.
7) Benefits, these are great ways to keep happy employees
   a. Health insurance
   b. 401(k) or SIMPLE IRA
   c. Disability insurance (long-term is cheap, and the employee pays for it.)

    d.   Dental or eye insurance

    e.   Days off, add birthdays and a floater, one everyone chooses

    f.   Flex hours, start and stopping times, but stick to a schedule

    g.   Bonus program, needs to be wolf proof (more later)

    h.   Review lunch, also include supervisor too if this is not a direct report

    i.   Supplemental insurance (employee pays for this as well)

8) Principles

    a.   If we don't take care of our clients, then somebody else will.

    b.   Treat your employees as family; you spend about the same amount of wake time with them as your own family.

    c.   Listen more than speak. A good listener is better than a good talker.

    d.   Keep emotions checked.

    e.   Do not raise your voice.

    f.   Offer a suggestion box.

    g.   Reward for time-and-money suggestions (by sharing savings). This also encourages new ideas.

    h.   When planning new products, include all who will make it happen, blue-sky ideas. Listen and list all. Then use a PE ratio analysis to evaluate.

    i.   Have themed days. This promotes a great atmosphere.

    j.   Have summer picnics, Christmas lunch, and, as mentioned, annual review lunches and brown-bag lunches. Sounds like a lot of eating but people open up when the bread is breaking.

    k.   Make sure you have an employee handbook with all company rules and guidelines. We give a free handbook template with this course, as well as many others.

    l.   Make sure everyone has access to this manual, as well as any other manuals such as quality.

m. All employees have the right to see their own personnel files in almost all states. This is law.

n. Employees are critical assets to the company and even more important than money itself. If you take care of your employees, they will take care of you!

Life Experience

We had a very large order that needed to be completed on time to meet a client's installation schedule. Needless to say, we were not looking too good to meet this schedule. I called all the employees together, told them we needed to get this order complete (was over 250 units), so we had a list of tasks that needed to be completed to get this job to the client on time. So each employee volunteered for the job. They felt they could do with the least amount of supervision and troubles. This included light assembly, making shipping boxes, labels, printing, folding, and inserting instruction manuals. I know this will not work in every situation; but in some aspects, it can. All products were inspected and tested prior to inserting into final packaging (the results: a happy client, employees feeling like part of the team and helping each other in a time of minor crisis). This has worked for me in many applications. This goes back to the US team. Even I, as the CEO, was out there inspecting, testing, and assembling!

CHAPTER 3

The Staff

Every shepherd has a solid staff. This helps as a tool to guide the sheep. A poor staff means lost sheep, get it? I know this is a metaphor but how true. The best-ran companies have a well-organized staff and one that is also well-balance. Don't be afraid to disagree. A good mix of right and left-brain thinking is very essential in a staff, just like the government republican and democrat. Just think if we had a one-party system, it almost becomes a dictatorship. A mix of minds produces creative thinking and a little competition and a successful company with happy employees and satisfied clients.

Every good shepherd has a solid staff.

> And take your Shepherd's staff with you,
> and use it to perform the miraculous signs I have
> shown you. (Exodus 4:17, NLT)

This was a command to Moses, and the point here is that the staff represents the support for the shepherd. Moses used the staff to perform miracles. Okay, I'm not guaranteeing that with a staff you are going to perform miracles; but with a good staff, you will perform very well.

How do I choose my staff?

When choosing a staff, you will want a group that shares your ideals but yet can complement areas that you yourself may be lacking. You, as a leader, also have specialized talents, and you cannot cover every area of the business. And the sooner you accept this, the sooner you are going to realize that you need to surround yourself with a solid staff. I have had the opportunity to build a business from the ground up. This goes from hiring the first employees all the way to building a staff.

In the beginning, you are small, and you really do not have much of an internal reporting structure. But as you grow, each employee will show their skills through work ethics and loyalty. Remember you are the one nurturing these values in each and every employee, so you are a part of the end results.

How do I spell staff?

S—Supporting. The role of the staff is to support the shepherd, the mission of the company, and mostly help support the flock.

T—Teach. Each staff member is a mentor and should be teaching and training for the successful future of the company.

A—Attitude. Each staff member is responsible for projecting positive attitudes. Nothing is more disturbing to an employee than seeing a manager with a bad attitude. This sends the wrong message and sets a poor example

F—Friendly. How can you do any of the above and not be friendly? This sometimes is hard to do all the time, but you need to realize this trait goes a long way with everyone. This trait is probably one of the most important.

F—Flexible. Not physically but supportively, you need to be open-minded and also be flexible to new ideas. You have to culture creativity, and this comes through flexibility.

Typically, the staff is meeting with the CEO/owner on a scheduled time and day. Each staff member has a responsibility for a part of the company. In larger corporations, this can be VPs, directors, and even managers. It is important that you meet and communicate. Your staff is also key in the planning process. This includes budgets, growth, cash flow (accounting), marketing, sales, employee requirements, promotions, and human relations (benefit review and structure).

> Work hard and become a leader, be lazy and
> become a slave. (Proverbs 12:24, NLT)

This shows that hard work will pay off, and the best workers become the best leaders. As a leader emerges from the flock, this is a ram, you need leaders, and you need help. Most importantly, good leaders emerge, no politics, no favoritism, just natural talent. A leader that emerges will most likely have the respect of the flock. A new leader moving in to the flock is not a bad thing, but it has a long learning curve and has to earn the respect of others. I am a true believer in emergence of leadership. I have had a lot more success through promotions of leaders than bringing in a leader from outside. Don't get me wrong though. There are many times you have to bring in new talent to help the company. I will discuss introducing a new ram into the flock, but first let's spell *ram*.

R—Ready. The leader has to be ready at any moment to handle the daily issues of a business, to do what it takes to satisfy clients and subordinates, to step up and take the challenge of daily issues.

A—Attitude. Reflects a positive attitude to all involved. People follow those who are positive and give their best. After all, who will perform well in a negative atmosphere?

M—Mentor. A good leader can recognize an up-and-comer and should mentor these skills. A good leader picks a team with people smarter than them (of course, in their fields). Mentoring is one of the most important traits of a leader; this is the passing of the knowledge. A leader that does not mentor will fail and could take the company down with them.

I have mentored many in my career and have had a great amount of success. Under my leadership, I have seen many of my associates move up in their careers, multiple entrepreneurs, corporate officers, and leaders in their industries. If you train people to understand what makes a company successful by you setting an example, this will have a "pay it forward" effect.

A ram is a leader and should be reflecting the shepherd principle. Your staff should be made up of rams. You should set a time aside at the beginning of each week with the staff. This should be done Monday morning but could be done near the end of the day on Friday. This is a huddle to go through the planning of the upcoming week, review any issues, and plan around them of fix them. This also should be a time to review any customer feedback (positive or negative) and to plan on sharing those with the flock.

The staff will help with the management process and should be held accountable for daily operations but also included in budgeting, planning for growth, and cash flow. There should be no secrets between staff or from the manager, none! This is what can take a company down in no time at all.

CHAPTER 4

Building the Flock

> If your gift is to encourage others, be encouraging. If it is giving, give generously. If God has given you leadership ability, take the responsibility seriously. And if you have a gift for showing kindness to others, do it gladly. (Romans 12:8, NLT)

Everyone has gifts (talents). As a shepherd, you need to be able to discover the gifts of your flock and help them to discover it for themselves. This will also help you set a course for their future in the company. There are many types of test out there you can give a new hire to discover their personality traits. These can also be used as tools to help everyone understand personalities and how you need to approach and work with people. One I found very useful and it is online free is the Myers-Briggs four-square personality test.

The Myers & Briggs Foundation can be found online at www.myersbriggs.org. This is a good and fun exercise that will allow each person in the company to discover their personality type. This is only effective if *everyone* takes this, including the CEO. This can be done as a lunch-provided exercise. The outcome from this is by sharing our personalities with each other, it is easier to understand the persons you are working with and their thought processes and core personality traits.

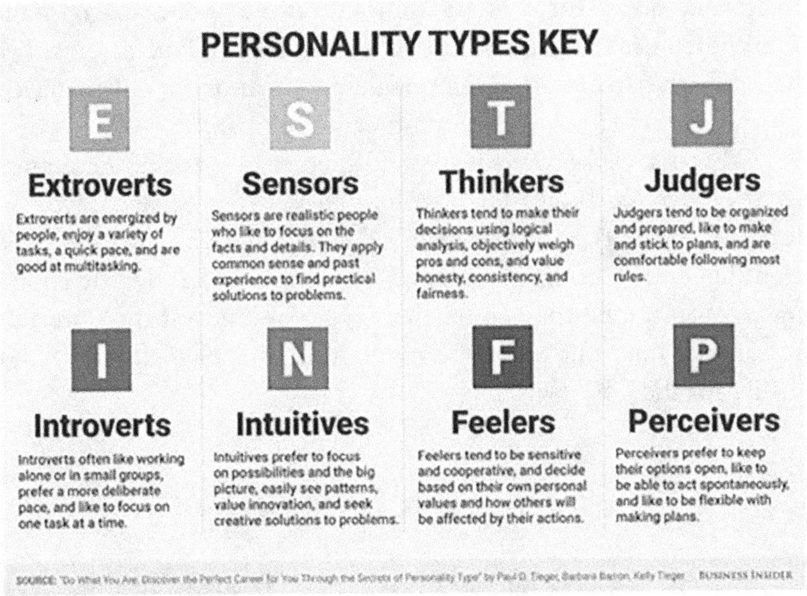
PERSONALITY TYPES KEY
E
Extroverts
Extroverts are energized by people, enjoy a variety of tasks, a quick pace, and are good at multitasking.
S
Sensors
Sensors are realistic people who like to focus on the facts and details. They apply common sense and past experience to find practical solutions to problems.
T
Thinkers
Thinkers tend to make their decisions using logical analysis, objectively weigh pros and cons, and value honesty, consistency, and fairness.
J
Judgers
Judgers tend to be organized and prepared, like to make and stick to plans, and are comfortable following most rules.
I
Introverts
Introverts often like working alone or in small groups, prefer a more deliberate pace, and like to focus on one task at a time.
N
Intuitives
Intuitives prefer to focus on possibilities and the big picture, easily see patterns, value innovation, and seek creative solutions to problems.
F
Feelers
Feelers tend to be sensitive and cooperative, and decide based on their own personal values and how others will be affected by their actions.
P
Perceivers
Perceivers prefer to keep their options open, like to be able to act spontaneously, and like to be flexible with making plans.
SOURCE: "Do What You Are: Discover the Perfect Career for You Through the Secrets of Personality Type" by Paul D. Tieger, Barbara Barron, Kelly Tieger
BUSINESS INSIDER

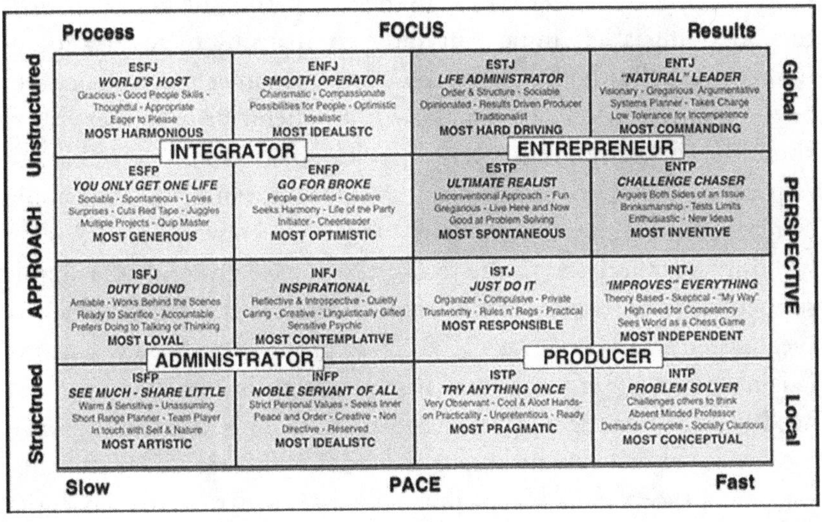
Process
FOCUS
Results
Unstructured
APPROACH
Structrued
Global
PERSPECTIVE
Local
ESFJ
WORLD'S HOST
Gracious - Good People Skills - Thoughtful - Appropriate Eager to Please
MOST HARMONIOUS
ENFJ
SMOOTH OPERATOR
Charismatic - Compassionate Possibilities for People - Optimistic Idealistic
MOST IDEALISTC
ESTJ
LIFE ADMINISTRATOR
Order & Structure - Sociable Opinionated - Results Driven Producer Traditionalist
MOST HARD DRIVING
ENTJ
"NATURAL" LEADER
Visionary - Gregarious Argumentative Systems Planner - Takes Charge Low Tolerance for Incompetence
MOST COMMANDING
INTEGRATOR
ENTREPRENEUR
ESFP
YOU ONLY GET ONE LIFE
Sociable - Spontaneous - Loves Surprises - Cuts Red Tape - Juggles Multiple Projects - Quip Master
MOST GENEROUS
ENFP
GO FOR BROKE
People Oriented - Creative Seeks Harmony - Life of the Party Initiator - Cheerleader
MOST OPTIMISTIC
ESTP
ULTIMATE REALIST
Unconventional Approach - Fun Gregarious - Live Here and Now Good at Problem Solving
MOST SPONTANEOUS
ENTP
CHALLENGE CHASER
Argues Both Sides of an Issue Brinksmanship - Tests Limits Enthusiastic - New Ideas
MOST INVENTIVE
ISFJ
DUTY BOUND
Amiable - Works Behind the Scenes Ready to Sacrifice - Accountable Prefers Doing to Talking or Thinking
MOST LOYAL
INFJ
INSPIRATIONAL
Reflective & Introspective - Quietly Caring - Creative - Linguistically Gifted Sensitive Psychic
MOST CONTEMPLATIVE
ISTJ
JUST DO IT
Organizer - Compulsive - Private Trustworthy - Rules n' Regs - Practical
MOST RESPONSIBLE
INTJ
"IMPROVES" EVERYTHING
Theory Based - Skeptical - "My Way" High need for Competency Sees World as a Chess Game
MOST INDEPENDENT
ADMINISTRATOR
PRODUCER
ISFP
SEE MUCH - SHARE LITTLE
Warm & Sensitive - Unassuming Short Range Planner - Team Player In touch with Self & Nature
MOST ARTISTIC
INFP
NOBLE SERVANT OF ALL
Strict Personal Values - Seeks Inner Peace and Order - Creative - Non Directive - Reserved
MOST IDEALISTC
ISTP
TRY ANYTHING ONCE
Very Observant - Cool & Aloof Hands-on Practicality - Unpretentious - Ready
MOST PRAGMATIC
INTP
PROBLEM SOLVER
Challenges others to think Absent Minded Professor Demands Compete - Socially Cautious
MOST CONCEPTUAL
Slow
PACE
Fast

I personally tested as an ENTP, as you can see from the chart. I fit the entrepreneur profile and also have a personal interest in technology and arts. This is pretty accurate since I have managed multiple companies in different roles and have twenty-four patents. I've owned, with partners, three companies. I was also in many manager, VP, and director roles in medium to large companies.

This is a well-proven and established testing system developed by the Myers & Briggs Foundation. These types of tests give you direction of the type of personality the new hire has and where the talent lies and to see if they are best suited to the job they are applying for. You can be charged for these types of test, but there are also free ones online. But I would only use this on the last few that best qualify for the job.

Lamb vs. Sheep

A lamb is a new hire and needs to be brought into the flock (company) with a love and compassion to help them grow into a sheep. They want to feel as though they are part of the flock and what they are doing is very important to the company. Remember, a receptionist is usually the first person a client/customer meets. They can be a direct reflection of what the visitor, client, or customer thinks about the company. A janitor, well, a clean place is a comfortable and respected place. Every employee plays an important role and should be reminded of this during reviews and even in conversations. A lamb will only learn as good as the teacher. So I have always had a simple rule: try to hire people with the same principles and philosophies or, even better, smarter than you! As a lamb grows into the new position (a lamb can even be a promoted into a new-position employee), they need to take ownership. This makes them feel needed and responsible. Once they take ownership and are doing their job correctly, they are now a sheep. As a sheep, they will take ownership of job duties and help to promote the mission of the company. Again, everyone is key to a successful company. If there is a job that is not key to the success of the company, is it really needed?

CHAPTER 5

The Lamb Principle (New Employee or Promoted Employee)

Hiring a new employee is a big decision and takes a lot of thought and interviewing. Although our laws do not permit certain personal questions, there are ways around this. You can't ask if someone attends church or what their spiritual life is about, but you can ask what they do on the weekends with their free time. What are your hobbies? How do you "recharge?" What are your favorite things to read? When you are faced with a problem, how do you tackle it? These are a few questions that can be asked that will tell you where their heart is.

New employees are like children. They watch, listen, and learn what happens in these first few months. Build the basic foundation of that employee for how the company runs. You need to be very specific and helpful during this period. What they learn during this time is building the basic principles that they will adhere to during their employment with you.

Here are my guidelines for the lamb principle:

L—Learn. A new employee will not only learn the job but all bout the company and the customers they serve. The more your employees learn, the smarter they become. And this enhances any company. Let them learn. Someday they will teach!

A—Aim. A good new employee will have personal goals to achieve. This is necessary for most people because they want to know they are going to grow in their job. Guess what, if they grow, so does the company.

M—Momentum. Hopefully forward, but a step backward once in a while is a good learning tool. As I have always said, it is okay to make a mistake as long as you learn from it. If you make the same mistake twice, guess what, you did not learn from your mistake.

B—Bring. Once a new employee is trained and integrated, they will *bring* results. The shepherd's job is to provide guidance in this process.

In your goals to have this lamb become a sheep, they must be set up with a good mentor. The mentor will help to build the lamb's confidence and support them during the learning process. A lamb will flourish if the learning process is done correctly. You will only get out what you put in; so the more time and energy you put into the lamb, the quicker they become a sheep.

CHAPTER 6

From a Lamb to a Sheep

A sheep can be defined as a seasoned loyal employee putting the goals of the company a head of one's own personal goals. Sound crazy? Well, if the goals of the company include the prospering of the whole, why not make the company successful to the best of their ability? A good sheep will have the following characteristics:

S—Selfless. This is putting the right decision first for the customer and the betterment of the company. It is not about me, sounds familiar. This takes a good shepherd to get this result from an employee. This is the most important trait to transform from lamb to sheep!

H—Helper. It is not my job! Not acceptable! Good employees will step in when needed. We need to encourage this. We are all servants to each other. If someone asks for help, they should get it. Sometimes companies get behind, and a good sheep will offer the extra help to get caught up. Problems arise. Good sheep will offer help to resolve the problems.

E—Enthusiastic. This is a good way to tell if an employee loves their job, period. I once had an employee ask me why this was called work when coming to my job is so fun! Now that's enthusiasm.

E—Entrepreneur. This is someone who can take on his or her job as they own it and want to grow it and make it better. Ownership: when an employee takes on this trait, stand back and watch the results. This must be encouraged. Each employee is the CEO of what they do. They are responsible to the plan, and they are responsible for their output.

P—Provider. This is the goal for a good sheep. A healthy sheep provides great wool, and a well-trained employee provides great results. This can be anything from a cheerful hello when answering the phone to a high-quality complex product and the best customer support.

The Nurturing Process, the Growing Process

I am the good shepherd; I know my sheep
and my sheep know me. (John 10:14)

Okay, do you know your sheep? Can you name everyone? Do you know any personal information, such as spouse, children, hobbies, or special skills? Do you share with the flock? Get out there. Get to know them. Walk around and talk. Believe me, if you show compassion, they will support you beyond expectations.

Get to Know Exercises

Have a lunch with the shepherd once a month. Talk hobbies, family; explore dreams of the company and the dreams of the employee. Have luncheon once a quarter. Invite employees to give feedback. Do not debate them. Just make notes and tell them you will address the concerns. Sometimes you will need to set up a one-on-one to talk depending on the concern. This is also a good time for you to share company plans, goals, and dreams.

Give a day off for their birthday. This is a special day, and why not let them celebrate it? Or get them a cake and in midafternoon celebrate with them and the other employees.

CHAPTER 7

Personality Types

Each of you should use whatever gift you
have received to serve other (1 Peter 4:10)

Okay, this is referring to gifts of the spirit. But this is a great guide, and we can intern for the sake of shepherding in a company. Let's use the term *talents* in substitution for *gifts*.

Each person is born with talents. Most discover these as they grow and mature. It is important as a shepherd to understand the talent of each person so we place and treat each person with respect according to the gifts they have. We also want to utilize these gifts so they keep the employee interested; and through this, it will help the company prosper!

I spent my career in product development and manufacturing. This takes a lot of specialized talent. This part of the book is an insert on technical personalities. It's really good to understand the technical mind. This is not from a psychiatrist point of view but forty-plus years of working with a managing multiple technical people. This is light and, in some ways, comedic, but it should offer some help when dealing with technical people and their sometimes-quirky personalities. This is an overview and should be used as a guide. Everyone is different, but certain personality traits are similar. This basically is a guide to help understand the technical mind and thought process. I creatively named these personalities in association with some stereotyping, but you will hopefully see the humor in this and help you recognize the personality as defined. This will also help you place this person and know how to approach and communicate with them.

Introduction

Blue-shirt club (this is what I call this group)

What is the blue-shirt club? Well, it relates to a dress code typically worn by techies. Most engineers will be wearing a light blue oxford with khaki pants or jeans when permitted. Why? This is not their area of expertise. A technical mind is thinking and exploring, not worrying what to wear. It is easier to go to a closet with two choices that do well together than to worry about how you are going to look, and who cares anyway? Now accessories are very important. Shoes must be functional and very comfortable. This usually means it is not going to be a fashion statement. But they will be able to stand on their feet for hours, if not days.

Belts must be able to support all belt-type accessories such as cell phone, PDA, GPS, and any other paging and beeping devices. And we cannot forget, they must hold up your pants as well. Usually one or two are all that is required. One black and one brown is all that is needed.

Pocket protectors, old school, this is legacy geek not usually seen today, now we see a smartphone strapped to their hip! The purpose of this is to help the world understand the technical mind. It is very often misunderstood; and in many cases, great relationships could have started but were never given a chance. So this is written in the personal pen of a technical mind that has worked at relationships and has also observed the different personalities that make up the technical world.

I also think that the blue-shirt club has all kinds of members. The engineer is one member; but this club also includes accountants, doctors, scientists, chemists, physicists, and patent attorneys, musicians, artists, and you get the idea.

Bill Gates once talked to a group of high school graduates and told them, "Be careful the next time you pick on one of the nerds in your class because it is very likely that you could be working for one them." So put down your stereotyping and open your mind and let's explore the technical mind. I think in the end, you will find that you will finally understand why we wear blue shirts

Main Personalities

This is an area that defines the whole concept and yet may seem simple by name but is very complex. Let's explore the basic personalities. We will start with the basic stereotypes with a good definition and then work to understand this personality. We are going to start with the most basic and work our way up to the more complex, so let's get going. Techies are broken down into three main categories, and from there, will call the other techie traits.

The *geek*. Into computers and the Internet, a geek is a person who is inordinately dedicated to and involved with the technology to the point of sometimes not appearing to be like the rest of us (non-geeks). Being a geek also implies a capability with the technology. Although historically, computer and Internet programming and hacking has been a male thing, there are now many girl geeks. The term *hacker* generally connotes competence more strongly than *geek* does.

Most geeks are somewhat argumentative, and you probably don't want to get into a discussion about a subject they are very familiar with. The discussion will go nowhere, and you will not get a word in. Most geeks will not argue about something they know very little about; but the next time you meet, they could be an expert as they will very likely research the subject, unless it is something totally uninteresting to them.

Geeks dress in many different ways. Most of them do not understand fashion and to the point that clothes are a necessity to cover nakedness. I have seen many geeks in clothes that were so wrinkled it looked like they left them in the dryer or in a heap for days, if not weeks. Most of them do not understand the gig line, the shirt seam, the belt buckle, and the fly zipper all lining up. I have seen this all over the place. They seem to be very emotional as well almost like they need to prove something. They do have a soft side though. They have a strong fascination with the opposite sex. Sometimes they go into the show-off mode when the opposite sex is around.

Also, geeks tend to wear their hair either really long (ponytail) or really short (buzzed). Some will have beards, and others will appear that they are trying to shave (missed spots). Older geeks can really get scary eye brows that are bushy, nose hair, and ear hair. Sometimes I think they are afraid of looking into a mirror. Scientifically, you want one on your team. They are passionate about what they do. This is what drives them, and failure is not in the equation.

The *nerd*. Traditionally, the designation *nerd* (occasionally in the form *nurd*) applies to an intellectually gifted (probably>120 or so IQ) but lonely and socially awkward person, one fascinated by knowledge, especially science and mathematics, and less interested in physical and social activities. Visual impairment (hence the glasses) and some form of high-functioning autism or Asperger's are also common characteristics, and the latter can often explain the social impairment.

Most nerds are really smart and are very quiet individuals. They are very intense when they are working on something and do not like to be disturbed. We call it getting into the zone. Most nerds like device technology, such as computers, PDAs, cell phone, stereos, and even automobiles in some cases, but usually from a restoring aspect or an engineering achievement, such as hybrid technology.

Nerds dress simple and typically are in the "blue shirt, khaki pants or jeans" range. Some iron and some don't, but no starch found here. The hair is usually worn longer than normal, but today what is normal? So let's leave it at the hair worn longer. Shoes are practical and may provide protection of some sort, either from weather or construction sites. However, they will be comfortable. You will rarely see a nerd in shorts or sandals.

Having a nerd on the team is a very positive move. They, however, need a quiet place to think and work. They can't socialize and work at the same time. They also will do a very complete job and can be very organized. A nerd can also get the job done if left alone. If they need something, they will seek it out.

Researcher. Research is an active, diligent, and systematic process of inquiry in order to discover, interpret, or revise facts, events, behaviors, or theories or to make practical applications with the help of such facts, laws, or theories. The term *research* is also used to describe the collection of information about a particular subject.

The researcher is one who loves to improve processes. This person can find the answer but may not know how to apply it. Typical research techies work in an R&D environment or as a patent attorney. They thrive on problem solving, prototyping, and advancing technology. The researcher however needs to hand off the formula to someone who can test and build it. They will move on to the next research project. They are usually very argumentative and do not like to be wrong. As similar to geek, they will research a subject and come back for the kill. You always picture a researcher in a white lab coat, and who knows what's under the coat? If you are a development company, you need a researcher, period!

Visionary. These are unique personalities, and many engineers possess some of this trait. But they who have this as a main personality are truly gifted; and almost all, if not all, successful companies have a visionary. This trait is truly a gift; it is sort of like a prophet or a wizard with a crystal ball. It is the ability to look into the future and see the needs of the market, the ability to enhance our world positively. Of course, not all products can be considered as positive enhancers to our world even though there is success. The best products, however, are the ones that will be around for a long time and will continue to improve and grow in market share; everyone will need or want one. Visionaries should lead the product development team, if not the whole company. Most companies have a visionary in the lead role of product development or technology depending on the type of company. Although visionaries are good leaders, they sometimes need help when it comes to the business side of things. History shows a great number of visionaries. Let's look at Leonardo da Vinci. He was the Einstein of the sixteenth century. He was an artist, a doctor, an engineer, and an author. Leonardo was intrigued by the universe, flight, and the human body. He is the perfect example of a visionary. We have many others just in the US (Thomas Edison, electricity for everyone; Henry Ford, the car; Bill Gates, the PC operating system; Steve Jobs, the iPod, iPhone, and the iPad; Lee Iacocca, changed the modern auto industry).

Chances are if you are a real company or if you have any chance of survival in this twenty-first century of producing products, you are or have a visionary. The traits of a visionary are similar to prophets from the old. They look at products today and look into the future, predicting needs and changes. These predictions sometimes can seem unbelievable but usually are pretty creditable. Tom Peters wrote a book in the early '80s called *Mega Trends* (he is a visionary). If you have not read this book, read it and see what he predicted for the future. It is scary but has two major predictions. First, the US would become an information society, and third-world countries would take over manufacturing. Did any of this come true?

Subcategories of Personalities (Traits)

The *grinder*. Used of or to a hacker, this term is a really serious slur on the person's creative ability; it connotes a design style characterized by primitive technique, rule-bounded, and brute force but a great amount of imagination. The grinder is the one that takes the research and proves it, can get it done, and even improve it, does not get caught up in detail and will have a proof of concept so quick it will make your head spin. This is what drives them, and this is what they do better than anything.

The grinder is an absolute when developing products. They will produce working prototypes without paying attention to all of the rules. This is what needs to be done when developing new products for the ever-changing market. Computers change daily! If you are not innovating, you are not on the market for long.

A grinder is somewhat unorganized, but order is present. They need lots of tools and usually money. This personality usually has been called *MacGyver*, as to the 80s show where he was always ingeniously rigging up some contraption to get out of a tight spot.

If there is a problem and you need a quick fix, call the grinder. He will get it up and running, but you will need to look for a long-term solution. They can't fit in the rules of normal corporations, but progressive companies need them and acknowledge this need, usually preferred to as the Skunk Works, but in a more positive swing the blue sky team!

The *polisher*. Hence, to refine, to wear off the rudeness, coarseness, or rusticity of, to make elegant and polite, as to polish life or manners. The grinder usually hands off to the polisher. The polisher will take the rough creation and bring it to a thing of beauty.

The polisher is extremely organized and adds order to a process. This is required to get a product to market. They set up all of the processes to get the finish line. If you do not have a polisher, you will always be a developer and not a producer. For some organizations, this works but not very many.

Polishers can lead, as well they are good at managing tasks and what needs to be done and who needs to do it. There are organizational polishers, and there are also process polishers. Typically, a polisher is not as creative as the grinder but brilliant at implementations.

Craftsman. A professional whose work is consistently of high quality, a creator of great skill in the manual arts, a skilled worker who practices some trade or handicraft. I think it goes without saying that many techies have this trait. I think some are much better craftsman than others, but it has some presence in all.

A craftsman can take an idea from a researcher and develop it into a work of beauty. This, of course, is trade related. Each person is gifted in specific areas that allow them to be very good at what they can do. This can be with minimal tools to an elaborate array of the finest tools (the second is more likely). The first is when this is all you have. A craftsman works best in a research or lab-type environment. They work at their own pace which is generally consistent and dependable. You cannot rush beauty. If you try, it will be a disappointment, and you may lose a craftsman.

For success here, support the craftsman and give them the tools and the money they need for all to be successful. Not all companies need a craftsman, but highly successful ones have more than one. They are the whole package (grinder and polisher) in one, but be careful on expectation and choosing because their craft is usually very niche.

Jack-of-all-trades. A person able to do a variety of different jobs acceptably well, this relates to being good but not great.

Craftsman-like characteristics but less refined and more flexible but still gets the job done, this person is capable of many talents and does all of them at different levels of skill, some great to others that are acceptable, none really bad. The jack knows what they can or can't do but also may know where to get help or assistance to get the job done. This trait is unique from the others, would compare to the doctor who is the "general practitioner," can diagnose and repair almost anything; but if it gets intense, you need a craftsman or a brain surgeon to help.

This trait also makes good leaders as well because they have a much broader vision and can see beyond the scope of the daily requirements. They typically are not real organized but know where and how to get information fast! Because of the broadness of capabilities, they are good at putting teams together and placing plans in place to get a job done.

Brain surgeon. One who is specific to a specialized highly technical field and usually has an MD, MS, or PhD in their title. This is a programmer, code writer, micro controller, firmware developer, microbiologist, physicist, etc. I think you get the idea. This is sky-high, cutting-edge research. These are the people that cure disease and develop ground-breaking technology. Every company does not need this capability; and if you do, get ready to pay.

These people are highly specialized and do not expect them to move beyond their specialty, or all will be disappointed. They also need a quiet environment to work, with a lot of tools and access to a technology source. With the Internet in place, this is now a breeze. They are good leaders of a focused group but not big-picture leaders; they can manage a portion of a project but not the entire project.

These people also end up in teaching careers because they are comfortable in a defined subject and typically the one of the better in that field

Rocket scientist: An endeavor requiring great intelligence or technical ability, a clever thinker; this is a trait that is associated with putting a man on the moon. This person is good as a problem solver, can think out of the box. The rocket scientist can lead a group but sometimes becomes too critical of others' work. There are industries that this is required, medical and aircraft manufacturing to name a few.

Most companies do not need a rocket scientist, as they are typically the types that find a way to do the impossible. Their personality, well, here is an example. Are you an optimist or a pessimist? Ask to the average person. Is the glass half full or half empty? The rocket scientists says, "Neither, the glass is too small." Emotions are out of the picture. We are talking about Spock-like personalities here.

If you are a leader in technology, no matter what, the field and you strive to be on the top of the cutting edge, you need a rocket scientist.

The *dreamer*. One that dreams of ways to improve anything, an idealist, a thinker, also can be impractical. This is similar to the visionary, and this type tends to waver outside of rules and sometimes reality. This, by no means, is a bad trait. This is the person you want in a blue sky meeting. (This is a "no holds barred" brainstorm session).

The *hawker*. He works directly with the sales organization to discover client requirements, develop solution strategies, and define technical capabilities. Usually this personality fits well in the makeup of getting a technical product to market. This person can be your best hope for supporting an engineered product in the field. I have seen the dress from flashy cutting edge to conservative blue shirt khaki pants.

A good sales engineer is a researcher, helping clients find the best solution or bringing the information back to be reviewed for feasibility and quoting. The sales engineer is able to support the customer and to provide training. If you have a technical product or service, this is the person you need to sell it and support it. An engineer can see right through a nontechnical sales person and to the point that they could even embarrass the salesman.

When you are working in a group with all of the personalities of the technical mind, it is good to have an understanding of how to approach and communicate with that personality. It is also good to understand how that personality can be used to the advantage of working with that personality. What is normal today? In the past and who knew what was in store for the future? If I look at the history of the United States, nerds are starting to rule the most powerful nation in the world. It doesn't stop there either. Look at Japan, Germany, Italy, Korea, China, India, and they are creeping into the Middle East (slowly).

If you look at the past one hundred years, we have done amazing things, from huge bridges to putting a man on the moon. The revolution started with the automobile, the assembly line, and mass production. This was the nuclei that started the technology race. We have become a society of one-upmanship," or "I can do it better, faster, and cheaper." Of course, this is only one approach. Another would be bigger, better, with more features. We are always trying to be the leader. Look at the history of the automobile. Ford, General Motors, and Chrysler are the USA's largest makers. Ford, through acquisitions, acquired Mercury and Lincoln, and General Motors the same for Chevrolet, Pontiac, Oldsmobile (now gone), Buick, and Cadillac, and we can't forget the Daewoo purchase. Also GM has a line of trucks that fall under the GMC moniker. Chrysler produces Dodge, Plymouth, and Jeep, and now they are owned by Daimler, the parent company of Mercedes. The same has happened in Germany, Italy, Japan, and will be soon in Korea.

Computers have taken the same path the big PC versus the Mac, has been around after beating out Commodore, Texas Instruments, Atari, and many other smaller attempts. Why is this happening? It is not because of accountants or businessmen but techies, dreamers, grinders, and polishers. Yes, a smart business man can harness this power and get it to the market and make millions, but it is the "blue-shirt club" that gets it created!

Today the race is technology (features and functions) in everything, but it all stems down to the root, the microchip basically in everything, and harnessing its power is only limited by the imagination. From an electric razor to a fighter jet, there is the presence of the microchip! Digital electronics has conquered the world. The new frontier revolves around this technology, more functions, more memory, faster operation, and smaller package. Our first PCs in the '80s typically were 10 MHz operating speed with 30 to 60 megabytes of hard drive and 256 to 512K of RAAM. Today approaching 5 GHz speed, 1 to 2 terabytes of hard drive and gigabytes of RAM, this is becoming a quick moving number. It goes up daily.

How does this happen? By teams of research, technical minded people (TMP), they all belong to the blue-shirt club.

Marketing vs. Research

Now with a little history behind us, we need to explore the evolution of a great product. We could pick many examples, but few are more interesting than the computer. Back in late 1981, the PC was born. It took the world by surprise. Who would believe that within twenty years, it would be almost as common as the TV? Microsoft was started with the 50K investment Bill Gates made with the purchase of the foundation to DOS (digital operating system), which was marketed to IBM; but the real mojo was kept for a version called MS-DOS, which Microsoft marketed to everyone. Now here is the interesting part. Most, if not all, nerds jumped on this one. It became the central focus of many of the techies' lives. The PC, along with Intel and Microsoft, took the *world* by storm. They left all competitors in the dust. The real competition went to equipment that made the best PC assembly; the rest was left to Intel and Microsoft.

There is always the best way to produce products. Do you produce products and look for markets or look for the market and produce the products? The most successful companies look for a market demand and produce a product to fill it. I have seen many products produced without a market demand, and they have failed miserably.

If you research a market and look for needs and wants, this will give you direction in which way you head in product development. One of the bigger failures that was not market driven that comes to mind is the 1985 Coke blunder. They introduced New Coke, a sweeter version to compete with Pepsi. Why did they fail? Because they pulled the old Coke off the shelf and replaced it with New Coke. This caused a mass rebellion among Coke drinkers, and Coke was forced to bring back Classic Coke. New Coke is gone! Pepsi has its follower, and Coke has theirs. New coke caused loyal Coke drinkers to abandon a long-time friend. Pepsi drinkers are also loyal to the brand and will typically not change. Coke lost large amounts of market.

Who listens to the market? Well, the car makers are since we are in the times of the baby boomers and most of these are now into their fifties. We are bringing back retro-designed cars. The Bug, Mustang, Charger, PT Cruiser, HHR, and Chevrolet are reintroducing the Camaro, and it is very similar in style to the 1960s version. Almost all manufacturers are producing a sporty two-seat model to cope with the midlife crisis situation. (I do not consider owning a sports car a midlife crisis. I look at picking up where we left off; however, there are those who would argue this.)

We could go on for amusing pages after pages of many examples of failed and great products; this is not the point. The point is listening to and knowing your market. Get the right team together to produce the products. Test the products with your market and listen to the feedback. Do this *fast*, or you will get surprised when you are not first to market.

Prior to developing products, know your customer and listen. Great products start with a need, and good products fulfill needs. Once you have a great market-driven idea for a product, you are now ready to assemble the team.

The Team

To develop the best product, you need the best team. A company is not a name. It is not a product; and least of all, it is a building. It is people; best companies have the best people. If you want to be a market leader, you need the best team, period! Let's look at a very old profession, shepherd. A shepherd sells wool. This comes from lambs; and to have the best wool, he needs the best lambs. To have the best lambs, he needs to nurture and take very good care of the lamb. He needs to keep them healthy and protect them. Now if a shepherd did not follow this simple plan, he loses. Poor wool means low prices and poor returns. You get the message. We need to be shepherds. We need to take care of our team. The team that is nurtured and supported and supplied with the best development tools will produce the best products. The best leaders are shepherds!

Okay, we have to start with the leader (our shepherd). Now that we have this defined, we need to assemble a product development team. Just look at this like a baseball team; all the players have different jobs to do, but they all have a common goal. This is to score. Each player has a position in the field and is critical to the team's success. Each player is put in his position based on his capabilities. The best teams have the best players in each role, but remember they all have the common role of scoring. You can have the best team in positions; but if they can't score, you will lose the game. Okay, how does this relate to a product team, you ask. Well, just as in the game of baseball, product development teams have positions, and they are unique. And if the team scores together, you will win in the marketplace.

CHAPTER 8

Rewarding a Job Well Done

People respond better to compliments. Give them often! Do you find it easier to criticize rather than compliment? I learned a long time ago you get better results complimenting versus criticizing. Take care of the flock, and it will serve you well. Serve your flock, and they will serve you. I think it is good to reward when there is success. The managers always get the big bonuses, and the workforce gets a small compensation comparative. Set the goals ahead of time. Make it known what can be earned to take the company to the next level. Most companies have the "we" team, the managers and the "they" team, the workforce. Don't we want the US team? We are always in this together; and we want a team that is one in unity, all working toward the same goal. Split teams create nonproductive agendas. What I am talking about is other things start to creep into the business, such as unions for example; this is a substitute shepherd for the ones that can't fulfill this need.

> Don't team up with those who are unbelievers. How can righteousness be a partner with wickedness? How can light live with darkness? (2 Corinthians 6:14 NLT)

Okay, this verse is talking about following God, but we can apply this to companies. You have to believe in the goals of the company, and you have to have faith in the leadership of the company. We have always used these terms in companies like "that employee really shines." We have also used the dark terms as well. "They seem lost in the dark." We need to have everyone believing in the company, the goals and the leadership. This makes for a successful company.

There are many things you can do to reward your sheep. Show them the benefits you provide and the value of them. Many sheep take benefits for granted because they do not understand their value. Let them be involved in the process of adding, changing, or removing benefits. This creates knowledge, ownership, and appreciation. In larger companies if the management loses relationship and respect of the employees, this opens the door for outside organizations, such as unions.

Here are great ways to reward and keep the flock meeting the goals of the company.

1) Share with the employee. Know the goals. Keep the goals posted on a bulletin board or website. You should show progress of the goals. This also helps you when you need to make adjustments to improve and reward when exceeding.
2) Involve the flock when choosing benefits.
3) Put together a reward program for job well done:
   a. Bonus program
   b. Extra time off
   c. Company stock
   d. Lunch with the shepherd
   e. A CEO award for outstanding performance beyond the call of duty
4) Meet and greet the flock daily.
5) Suggestion box. If it saves the company money, share the savings as a reward.

Remember this is your greatest asset, taking care of them, and they will take care of you and the company. I know I am repeating this, but it is too important to say only once.

CHAPTER 9

Conflict

What do you think? If a Shepherd owns a
hundred sheep, and one of them wanders away,
will he not leave the ninety-nine on the hills
and go to look for the one that wandered off?
—Matthew 18:12

Guidance not Criticism

A positive comment goes ten times further than one negative. It is so easy to criticize, but why is it so difficult to complement? Why can't we compliment to correct? Hmmm, this seems like a weird concept. Wow! I just love the way you attempted to increase speed, but is it not better to operate a little slower and have less fallout?

Note: when having a conversation with a person of the opposite sex, it is always good to do this in an area or office with windows; or if not, invite another person (staff or supervisor) of the same sex. If neither of those are an option, I would just leave the door to the office ajar or partly open. This is a good practice any time you are having a conversation with an employee.

Here is the 1,2,3 concept for a correction:

Step 1: Give the employee a chance to correct the errors in their own way. Let them come up with a solution. This can be anything such as tardiness to getting along with other employees to productivity issues. If this works, sit with them and thank them for working out a solution. If this does not work, next step.

Step 2: Ask the employee to come and have a conversation with you. This will be the time when you will assist the employee with a workable solution. This should also be noted that there was an issue with the solution. The employee tried, and it did not work. This should also be explained why it did not work, and this is an opportunity for the two of you to work together and come up with an agreeable solution. Again, if this works, thank them for putting the effort into working with you and resolving the issue. If this does not work, next step.

Step 3: Now be for we talk about this step. You should have documented steps 1 and 2 into the employees' file, and you can have them even sign it as documented proof you had these discussions. Discharging an employee is a very difficult thing to do, but there are times it has to be done. There are many reasons for this, and some can be immediate discharge for things such as disorderly conduct, stealing, or harming another person. But we are talking here about someone who just can't work out an issue that is causing problems that are not conducive to the smooth operation of the company. If you have to release an employee, you should always do it with another manager/supervisor. This is for three basic reasons:

1) A witness in case any legal action is taken (this is rare but has to be considered).
2) For protection in rare cases, this causes rage and employee gets abusive either with language or physical force. With an additional person, this would rarely happen.

3) This is another step that always should be followed. If it is a woman to be discharged, the second person should be another woman; and likewise, if it is a man, then the second person should be a man too. I understand in some cases this is not possible, but if you can do this, you will most like not have any issues further down the road. The second person should always be a staff manager or a supervisor.

But three strikes, you are out.

Life Experience

I have released people due to unethical work habits and sadly in major downturns in the economy, which I had to reduce to match our cash flow. This is, by far, the hardest thing I have had to do in a company. You are basically releasing someone who you and they have invested a lot of time in. A good example of the 1, 2, 3 method is a story of a young man who was a good producer but had anger issues. He would get into shouting matches with other employees, and I would get complaints. So I sat down with this young gentleman, and we had a discussion about his anger issues. After a talk, me explaining that other employees were fearing him and did not want to work with him, he told me that he would apologize and make it right and control his temper. Well, a few weeks went by, and he exploded again and had another female employee in tears. So now my second talk, I got him to agree to visit with a therapist once a week until the problem was under control, and I agreed and assured him this was the only way he would continue to work here. He agreed to the therapy, and the company paid for it. Well, things seemed to be going well for the next few months until one day, he got into an argument with our quality manager. He took the product he was working on and threw into the wall, and it stuck in the dry wall. Okay, this was strike three, and he was putting other employees in risk of harm. I called the HR manager. And we sat down with the young man and told him he was being released from the company, and he would get his final paycheck when we received all of his uniforms. Now we thought this was done. He walked out, was gone for about one hour when he came back. He came into my office and threw a bag of his uniforms on my desk. Okay, this was a concern for me. Fortunately, the supervisor from the shop followed him in. I informed him that he would get his last paycheck, but there would be no severance pay. He then was promptly escorted out. And in the meantime, someone called 911, and the police was there during the escort. Not every discharge goes this way. This young man had real anger issues. Why did I work so hard to help him? He was a good worker and was fast and accurate. He was worth the effort. Unfortunately, he could not get the anger in check, so we had to discharge him as there was a risk of injury and other employees leaving because of him. On a positive note, the other employees say that I really cared and tried to help. This gave them comfort.

CHAPTER 10

Accountability

> To those who use well what they are given,
> even more will be given, and they will have abun-
> dance. But from those who do nothing, even
> what little they have will be taken away. (Mathew
> 25:29)

Everyone is accountable! You are responsible for your work to be complete on time and highest of quality. This is always the way to run a company. Accountability is not only needed to correct an issue but also gives the employee pride in what they do. Would they sign their name on their work? Would they be proud of their accomplishments? At the end of the day, it is the shepherd that is accountable for all the flock. On the other hand, ignoring accountability will also have consequences, as described in chapter 9.

Remember, President Truman said, "The buck stops here." What he means is ultimately, as president, he is responsible for the operation of the United States. Well, the same goes for every CEO and manager/supervisor in any company, so it is very important to have employees that are willing to be fully accountable for the work they perform in the company. So at the end of the day, the person managing the company, the shepherd, is the most accountable for the success of the company.

So accountability goes always to the top, so it is up to the shepherd to keep the team onboard with accountability. We are also accountable to our clients. Remember the saying "The customer is always right." What this means is if there is an issue according to the customer, whether real or perceived, it still is a problem and needs to be resolved to keep this client coming back. Again, if we do not take care of our customers, someone else will. Also having a good quality plan, company handbook, and third-party observation are good ways to maintain accountability. Later we will talk about these types of programs.

CHAPTER 11

Focusing

Inward Focused vs. Outward Focused

Christ gives a real great example of this. I can't think of a better example. He had twelve disciples, and they were in training to reach the main goal, which was to save all of humanity from sin and to follow Christ's teachings and be rewarded with eternal life in heaven. So Christ was very focused on his small group to teach them on the ways to reach out to all of humanity. This was the inward focus, but the goal to reach out to all was the outward focus.

> Jesus called out to them (the disciples),
> "Come, follow me, and I will show you how to
> fish for people!" (Matthew 4:19 NLT)

You need them both. One will not work alone. So let's look at this for a company. You must train your flock to meet the ultimate goals of the company. You need to properly train them in every aspect of what you expect them to do. If you fail in this, you will fail in your ultimate goal. So let's define inward versus outward: inward focus is making sure all of the flock is on the same goal to provide what is needed of them to reach the ultimate goal of the company.

Let's look at some examples:

1) Employee training
2) Employee meetings to share the achievements with everyone
3) Regular reviews of progress
4) Lunch and learn
5) Rewarding accomplishments
6) Provide a bonus program that has goals to meet, including the overall success of the company
7) Quality programs such as ISO 9000 or Six Sigma
   a. ISO 9000 is a series of standards, developed and published by the International Organization for Standardization (ISO), that define, establish, and maintain an effective quality assurance system for manufacturing and service industries.
   b. Six Sigma certification is a confirmation of an individual's capabilities with respect to specific competencies. Just like any other quality certification, however, it does not indicate that an individual is capable of unlimited process improvement—just that they have completed the necessary requirements from the company granting the certification.

Note: both of the above programs are excellent in maintaining great control of quality and continuous improvement, but this really is designed toward manufacturing and medium to larger-size companies. Even if you do not have either of these two systems in place, you should still develop a quality control system with a manual. When you are large enough to be able to support a certified system as described above, you will be more than halfway there.

Outward focus is achieving the ultimate goal of the company.

Let's look at some examples:

1) Advertising
2) Allowing an easy path for customer feedback
3) Well-written communications

4) Physically talking to clients either in person or by phone
5) Documenting any obligation approved by you and your client
6) Great reception and follow-up service.
7) Written pricing, warranty, service, and return policies.
8) Keeping clients informed on product changes or issues found. In the auto industry, they refer to this as a *recall*.
9) And as stated, a good quality system

To have good outward focus, you must also have good inward focus. These two need to be balanced. Too much of one or the other will destroy a company. Remember the examples in the beginning. Enron was so focused on meeting the needs of the stockholders. They falsified balance sheets to try and make stockholders happy, too much inward focus.

GM buried themselves in retirement commitments and could not meet the demands of required cash flow, which resulted in multiple failures, including quality, and resulting in Chapter 13 bankruptcy and government bailout. This was too inward focused.

The banks gave loans with little or no down payment required to people that could not make the monthly payments in the time allotted, again failure and government bailout. This was too outwardly focus.

CHAPTER 12

No Final Word but Good News

Rules to follow:

1) Set a company goal or mission
2) Hire employees that you feel will make a great contribution to the company
3) Do panel interviews. What is that, you may ask. Have all of the managers and supervisors, along with HR (human resources), interview all together. This works out real well because everyone gets to hear the same story. One-on-one interviews are long and tedious, not only for the interviewee but also the company as a whole. Also, you end up with long meetings after the interview, discussing what each person heard. With a panel interview, after the interviewee leaves, the discussion to hire or move on is a much simpler process.
4) Prior to an interview, agree on what question to ask. (I have included a real nice set of questions you can and cannot ask.)
5) Make sure you have all of your policies and rules written into an employee handbook. After hiring, give this to them and explain they need to read it and bring back the signed page, as a commitment that they read it, and explain this will go into the file.

6) Keep a company file on every employee.
7) Reward employees for jobs well done.
8) Keep open communications with your customers.
9) This one is hard to swallow but remember this: the customer is always right.
10) Also if you do not take care of your customers, some other company will be glad to.
11) Also if you do not take care of the flock, another company will be glad to. Just remember the 99 (Matthew 18:12).

In closing, I have included documentation that will help during the interview process, starting of employee records, and a solid foundation for an employee handbook.

Follow this shepherd theory, and you will have a successful company/career.

> Be shepherds of God's flock that is under your care, serving as overseers—not because you must, but because you are willing, as God wants you to be; not greedy for money, but eager to serve. (1 Peter 5:2)

THE INTERVIEWING PROCESS

A word about interviewing, it has been said that hiring an employee is a million-dollar decision. Yes, it is, if you consider pay, benefits, time off, output quality, and the ability to support the company efforts.

I have compiled list of questions to help you recognize the proper traits of a potential employee to see if they are a good fit for the company and the company is a good fit for them. Also included are questions you cannot ask per the right to work laws. But I will also give you alternatives and work around questions that you can ask that basically go down a similar path.

Also I am in favor of a panel review. This is having everyone that should be involved in the interviewing process all together during the interviewing process. This process allows everyone to hear and share the questions and answers that are discussed. This also cuts down on time for the potential employees' visit, and there will be nothing said or promised that everyone didn't hear.

Questions to ask at an interview:

Teamwork

For questions like these, you want a story that illustrates the ability to work with others under challenging circumstances.

Think team conflict, difficult project constraints, or clashing personalities.

1. Talk about a time when you had to work closely with someone whose personality was very different from yours.
2. Give me an example of a time you faced a conflict while working on a team. How did you handle that?
3. Describe a time when you struggled to build a relationship with someone important. How did you eventually overcome that?
4. We all make mistakes we wish we could take back. Tell me about a time you wish you'd handled a situation differently with a colleague.
5. Tell me about a time you needed to get information from someone who wasn't very responsive. What did you do?

Client-Facing Skills

If the role you're interviewing for works with clients, definitely be ready for one of these. Find an example of a time where you successfully represented your company or team and delivered exceptional customer service.

1. Describe a time when it was especially important to make a good impression on a client. How did you go about doing so?
2. Give me an example of a time when you did not meet a client's expectation. What happened, and how did you attempt to rectify the situation?
3. Tell me about a time when you made sure a customer was pleased with your service.
4. Describe a time when you had to interact with a difficult client. What was the situation, and how did you handle it?
5. When you're working with a large number of customers, it's tricky to deliver excellent service to them all. How do you go about prioritizing your customers' needs?

Ability to Adapt

Times of turmoil are finally good for something! Think of a recent work crisis you successfully navigated. Even if your navigation didn't feel successful at the time, find a lesson or silver lining you took from the situation.

1. Tell me about a time you were under a lot of pressure. What was going on, and how did you get through it?
2. Describe a time when your team or company was undergoing some change. How did that impact you, and how did you adapt?
3. Tell me about the first job you've ever had. What did you do to learn the ropes?
4. Give me an example of a time when you had to think on your feet in order to delicately extricate yourself from a difficult or awkward situation.
5. Tell me about a time you failed. How did you deal with this situation?

Time Management Skills

In other words, get ready to talk about a time you juggled multiple responsibilities, organized it all (perfectly), and completed everything before the deadline.

1. Tell me about a time you had to be very strategic in order to meet all your top priorities.
2. Describe a long-term project that you managed. How did you keep everything moving along in a timely manner?
3. Sometimes it's just not possible to get everything on your to-do list done. Tell me about a time your responsibilities got a little overwhelming. What did you do?
4. Tell me about a time you set a goal for yourself. How did you go about ensuring that you would meet your objective?

5. Give me an example of a time you managed numerous responsibilities. How did you handle that?

Communication Skills

You probably won't have any trouble thinking of a story for communication questions since it's not only part of most jobs, it's part of everyday life. However, the thing to remember here is to also talk about your thought process or preparation.

1. Give me an example of a time when you were able to successfully persuade someone to see things your way at work.
2. Describe a time when you were the resident technical expert. What did you do to make sure everyone was able to understand you?
3. Tell me about a time when you had to rely on written communication to get your ideas across to your team.
4. Give me an example of a time when you had to explain something fairly complex to a frustrated client. How did you handle this delicate situation?
5. Tell me about a successful presentation you gave and why you think it was a hit.

Motivation and Values

A lot of seemingly random interview questions are actually attempts to learn more about what motivates you. Your response would ideally address this directly even if the question was not explicit about it.

1. Tell me about your proudest professional accomplishment.
2. Describe a time when you saw some problem and took the initiative to correct it rather than waiting for someone else to do it.

3. Tell me about a time when you worked under close supervision or extremely loose supervision. How did you handle that?
4. Give me an example of a time you were able to be creative with your work. What was exciting or difficult about it?
5. Tell me about a time you were dissatisfied in your work. What could have been done to make it better?

Questions you can't ask in an interview:

Nationality

Certainly, you want to be sure that a candidate can legally work for you, but it's important to be careful how you ask. These questions address citizenship, language, and other touchy subjects.

1. What you can't ask: are you a US citizen? Although this seems like the simplest and most direct way to find out if an interviewee is legally able to work for your company, it's hands off. Rather than inquiring about citizenship, question whether or not the candidate is authorized for work. What to ask instead: are you authorized to work in the US?
2. What you can't ask: what is your native tongue? Finding out about a candidate's native language may seem like a good way to find out about their fluency, but you may offend applicants that are sensitive to common assumptions about their language. Additionally, as an employer, it's not your concern how the applicant attained fluency in a language—just that they are fluent. What to ask instead: what languages do you read, speak, or write fluently?
3. What you can't ask: how long have you lived here? Familiarity with local culture may be important to the position, but it's important not to ask about a candidate's residency in the

country or region directly. Rather, ask about their current situation, and they may volunteer information about their past along the way. What to ask instead: what is your current address and phone number? Do you have any alternative locations where you can be reached?

Religion

Religion is a subject that should be treaded upon lightly at the office, and even more so in interviews. Protect yourself from overstepping the boundaries but still get the information you need with these questions.

1. What you can't ask: what religion do you practice? You may want to know about religious practices to find out about weekend work schedules, but it's imperative that you refrain from asking directly about a candidate's beliefs. Instead, just ask directly when they're able to work, and there will be no confusion. What to ask instead: what days are you available to work?

2. What you can't ask: which religious holidays do you observe? Again, scheduling is important, but don't risk stepping on toes to find out what you need to know. Simply confirm that your interviewee can work when you need them to. What to ask instead: are you able to work with our required schedule?

3. What you can't ask: do you belong to a club or social organization? This question is too revealing of political and religious affiliations, and candidates are not required to share such information with potential employers. Additionally, this question has little to no relation to a candidate's ability to do a job. For this question, it's important that the wording focuses on work. What to ask instead: are you a member of a professional or trade group that is relevant to our industry?

Age

Maturity is essential for most positions, but it's important that you don't make assumptions about a candidate's maturity based on age. Alternately, you have to be careful about discrimination toward applicants nearing retirement. These questions will keep you in the clear.

1. What you can't ask: how old are you? While it seems like a simple question, it's in fact quite loaded. Knowledge of an applicant's age can set you up for discrimination troubles down the road. To be safe, just ensure that the candidate is legally old enough to work for your firm. What to ask instead: are you over the age of eighteen?

2. What you can't ask: how much longer do you plan to work before you retire? Again, asking this question opens up discrimination troubles. While you may not want to hire an older worker who will retire in a few years, you can't dismiss an applicant for this reason. Instead, see what the candidate's plans are for the future; they may plan to work for a number of years. What to ask instead: what are your long-term career goals?

Marital and Family Status

These questions primarily concern women with children, but they're applicable to everyone. Ensure that you don't make assumptions, and avoid embarrassing candidates by using the following questions.

1. What you can't ask: is this your maiden name? This question, like many others, may seem innocent and simple, but it's off-limits. A woman's marital status isn't something that's required to be shared with employers. Instead, verify whether or not she's gained experience using any other

names. What to ask instead: have you worked or earned a degree under another name?

2. What you can't ask: do you have or plan to have children? Clearly, the concern here is that family obligations will get in the way of work hours. Instead of asking about or making assumptions on family situations, get to the root of the issue by asking directly about the candidate's availability. What to ask instead: are you available to work overtime on occasion? Can you travel?

3. What you can't ask: can you get a babysitter on short notice for overtime or travel? Don't make the mistake of assuming that a candidate has children or that they don't already have proper childcare plans. As with many other questions, the key here is to ask directly about availability. What to ask instead: you'll be required to travel or work overtime on short notice. Is this a problem for you?

4. What you can't ask: do you have kids? This one is for positions in which the candidate may work with children. The added experience of children at home may be a bonus for you, but it's not an employer's place to ask about this. Rather, inquire about the candidate's experience, and they may volunteer this information to you anyway. What to ask instead: what is your experience with "x" age group?

5. What you can't ask: who is your closest relative to notify in case of an emergency? Although not especially offensive, this question makes assumptions about the candidate's personal life. They may not be close to relatives and instead prefer to list a friend or caretaker. What to ask instead: in case of emergency, who should we notify?

6. What you can't ask: what do your parents do for a living? Asking a candidate about their parents can reveal a lot, but it's not directly related to their future performance in a position. However, if you are trying to find out if your candidate's family has traditionally worked in your industry, this question is a good way to find out. What to ask instead: tell me how you became interested in the "x" industry.

7. What you can't ask: if you get pregnant, will you continue to work, and will you come back after maternity leave? Ultimately, you want to invest your time in a candidate that will stick around, but you can't ask a woman to share her pregnancy plans, or lack thereof, with you. Discuss her general plans for the future to gauge her commitment level, baby or not. What to ask instead: what are your long-term career goals?

Gender

Once you've reached the interview stage, a candidate's gender is almost always clear. It is important, however, to ensure that you don't make assumptions about a person's abilities based on this information.

1. What you can't ask: we've always had a man/woman do this job. How do you think you will stack up? Leave gender out of this question, and you should be fine. Inquire about the applicant's ability to handle the job, but don't ask directly about how being a man or woman could affect it. What to ask instead: what do you have to offer our company?

2. What you can't ask: how do you feel about supervising men/women? This question, although it may seem like a valid concern, is not acceptable. The candidate may not have any issues working with the opposite or same sex, and you'll seem crass for even bringing it up. What to ask instead: tell me about your previous experience managing teams.

3. What you can't ask: what do you think of interoffice dating? The practice of interoffice dating can be distracting, break up teams and cause a number of other problems in the workplace. But asking this question makes assumptions about the candidate's marital status and may even be interpreted as a come-on. What to ask instead: have you ever been disciplined for your behavior at work?

Health and Physical Abilities

Your employees' health and abilities may be essential to getting the job done, but it's important to avoid assumptions and discrimination. Stick to these questions in order to avoid embarrassment and legal troubles.

1. What you can't ask: do you smoke or drink? As an employer, you probably want to avoid someone who has a drinking problem or will take multiple smoke breaks throughout the day. It's even a concern for insurance. Instead of asking about this directly, find out if they've had trouble with health policies in the past. What to ask instead: in the past, have you been disciplined for violating company policies forbidding the use of alcohol or tobacco products?

2. What you can't ask: do you take drugs? This question is just a simple confusion of terms. Your interviewee may think you're asking about prescription drugs, which is off-limits. Make sure you specify that you want to know about illegal drug use instead. What to ask instead: do you use illegal drugs?

3. What you can't ask: how tall are you? In a labor environment, height may be essential to the job, but this question is too personal. As with many of these questions, it's best just to ask directly about the candidate's ability to do what's required of them. What to ask instead: are you able to reach items on a shelf that's five feet tall?

4. What you can't ask: how much do you weigh? This highly personal question is embarrassing for most and is not necessarily relevant to a candidate's ability to do even a physical-labor job. Avoid making assumptions, and ask about abilities directly. What to ask instead: are you able to lift boxes weighing up to fifty pounds?

5. What you can't ask: how many sick days did you take last year? No one wants a flaky employee, but even the most dedicated workers get sick every now and then. Take a look

at missed days as a whole to measure the candidate's commitment. What to ask instead: how many days of work did you miss last year?

6. What you can't ask: do you have any disabilities? Disabilities, whether they're physical or mental, may affect a candidate's ability to do the job, but it's critical that you avoid asking about them. Rather, find out if the applicant can handle doing what's required. What to ask instead: are you able to perform the specific duties of this position?

7. What you can't ask: have you had any recent or past illnesses or operations? Again, gauging commitment is important, but illness isn't something that most people can help. The answer here is to make sure that the candidate can perform the job while avoiding questions about his or her physical abilities. What to ask instead: are you able to perform the essential functions of this job with or without reasonable accommodations?

Miscellaneous

Avoid interviewing gaffes by sidestepping these questions about residence, legal troubles, and military service.

1. What you can't ask: how far is your commute? Although hiring employees who live close by may be convenient, you can't choose candidates based on their location. Find out about their availability instead. What to ask instead: are you able to start work at 8:00 a.m.?

2. What you can't ask: do you live nearby? If your candidate lives outside of the city your company is hiring in, it may be necessary to have them move to your area. But again, you can't discriminate based on location. Rather, find out if the applicant is willing to move closer to the office. What to ask instead: are you willing to relocate?

3. What you can't ask: have you ever been arrested? In sensitive positions, like those that deal with money, you may

want to find out about your candidate's legal fortitude. But
ensure that you ask only directly about crimes that relate
to your concern. What to ask instead: have you ever been
convicted of "x" (fraud, theft, and so on)?

4. What you can't ask: were you honorably discharged from
the military? A bad military record can be illuminating,
but you can't ask about it. Instead, ask about the candidate's experience, and they may volunteer this information
on their own. What to ask instead: tell me how your experience in the military can benefit the company.

5. What you can't ask: are you a member of the National
Guard or Reserve? Losing an employee to military service
can be disrupting, but it's critical that you don't discriminate based on assumptions of a candidate's upcoming military commitments. What to ask instead: find out what
their plans are for the short term instead.

THE SHEPHERD PRINCIPLE

Job Performance Review Guide New Higher (Lamb)

Employee

Employee Name		Review Period	
Department		Manager	

Performance goals and objectives

0 to 2 months	2 to 4 months	4 to 6 months
−Become familiar with your department's business goals. −Work with your manager to define and document your goals. Include what you are expected to produce by your first review, activities needed to accomplish results, and success criteria.	−Make certain defined goals and criteria are realistic. Renegotiate if necessary. −Are you focusing your time on the goals you committed to? If not, either work with your manager to change your goals or reevaluate how you spend your time.	−Review performance goals to see if you are on target. Reprioritize work accordingly.
Notes/Actions		

Skills and knowledge development

0 to 2 months	2 to 4 months	4 to 6 months
–Understand the specific skills and knowledge you need. Use the job profile as your guide. –Build a skill development plan based on the goals agreed to by you and your manager. –Complete the new administrator orientation.	–Attend one of the sessions in the administrator certification program. See the training resource site for courses. –Review your development plan and suggested curriculum for additional skills and training.	–Attend at least one more session in the administrator certification program. –Create a timeline with associated tasks that you will follow in order to attain the skills outlined in your personal development plan.
Notes/Actions		

Processes and methods

0 to 2 months	2 to 4 months	4 to 6 months
–Familiarize yourself with work processes and methods used in your job. Be clear on who owns those processes and how you can support process goals. –Set clear timelines for task due dates. Keep timelines up to date.	–Identify and eliminate unnecessary variation in the way you perform work processes. –Ensure that your work responsibilities are clear, defined, and realistic.	–Get to know the people who work cross-functionality in common work processes. –Seek to simplify any work processes in order to cut cycle time.
Notes/Actions		

Feedback

0 to 2 months	2 to 4 months	4 to 6 months
–Understand the different types of feedback and the ways in which you will receive feedback.	–Are you getting the feedback you need? Is feedback timely, specific, and frequent? –Compare actual performance and expected performance.	–Are you giving feedback to others who need it? –Compare actual and expected performance.
Notes/Actions		

The Shepherd Theory
EMPLOYEE HANDBOOK

Release date: xx/xx/xxxx

CONTENTS

SECTION 1

Welcome

1.1 History, goals, and culture

1.2 Purpose of this handbook

This handbook has been prepared to inform new employees of the policies and procedures of this company and to establish the company's expectations. It is not all-inclusive or intended to provide strict interpretations of our policies; rather, it offers an overview of the work environment. This handbook is not a contract, expressed or implied, guarantying employment for any length of time and is not intended to induce an employee to accept employment with the company.

The company reserves the right to unilaterally revise, suspend, revoke, terminate, or change any of its policies, in whole or in part, whether described within this handbook or elsewhere, in its sole discretion. If any discrepancy between this handbook and current company policy arises, conform to current company policy. Every effort will be made to keep you informed of the company's policies; however, we cannot guarantee that notice of revisions will be provided. Feel free to ask questions about any of the information within this handbook.

This handbook supersedes and replaces any and all personnel policies and manuals previously distributed, made available or applicable to employees.

1.3 At-will employment

Employment at this company is at will. An at-will employment relationship can be terminated at any time, with or without reason or notice by either the employer or the employee. This at-will employment relationship exists regardless of any statements by office personnel to the contrary. Only [enter authorized person's name] is authorized to modify the at-will nature of the employment relationship, and the modification must be in writing.

This section should welcome the new employee and introduce them to the character of the company. Write briefly about how the company began and who is in charge. Describe the company's goals, philosophy, and core principles. Avoid describing the company like a family as that might imply indefinite employment.

Sections 1.2 and 1.3 are essential items for a handbook. Employers are vulnerable to lawsuits if they do not provide statements regarding the noncontractual nature of the handbook or at-will employment. Employees should also agree to these terms on the Acknowledgment of Receipt form. Some states limit the terms of at-will employment; so consult with an employment attorney regarding your state's laws.

SECTION 2

Workplace Commitments

2.1 Equal opportunity employment

This company is an equal opportunity employer and does not unlawfully discriminate against employees or applicants for employment on the basis of an individual's race, color, religion, creed, sex, national origin, age, disability, marital status, veteran status, or any other status protected by applicable law. This policy applies to all terms, conditions, and privileges of employment, including recruitment, hiring, placement, compensation, promotion, discipline, and termination.

Whenever possible, the company makes reasonable accommodations for qualified individuals with disabilities to the extent required by law. Employees who would like to request a reasonable accommodation should contact [enter authorized person's name].

Several laws enforced by the US Equal Opportunity Employment Commission prohibit workplace discrimination. The Americans with Disabilities Act requires employers to provide, among other things, reasonable accommodations to qualified individuals with disabilities unless to do so would cause an undue hardship to the company. Include an equal opportunity statement and a disability statement to exhibit that your company observes these laws. The company should be aware of state and/or local laws which provide greater protection than the federal discrimination laws, such as recognizing additional protected classes beyond those protected by federal statute.

2.2 Nonharassment policy/nondiscrimination policy

This company prohibits discrimination or harassment based on race, color, religion, creed, sex, national origin, age, disability, marital status, veteran status, or any other status protected by applicable law. Each individual has the right to work in a professional atmosphere that promotes equal employment opportunities and is free from discriminatory practices, including without limitation harassment. Consistent with its workplace policy of equal employment opportunity, the company prohibits and will not tolerate harassment on the basis of race, color, religion, creed, sex, national origin, age, disability, marital status, veteran status or any other status protected by applicable law. Violations of this policy will not be tolerated.

Discrimination includes but is not limited to making any employment decision or employment related action on the basis of race, color, religion, creed, age, sex, disability, national origin, marital, or veteran status, or any other status protected by applicable law.

Harassment is generally defined as unwelcome verbal or non-verbal conduct, based upon a person's protected characteristic, that denigrates or shows hostility or aversion toward the person because of the characteristic, and which affects the person's employment opportunities or benefits, has the purpose or effect of unreasonably interfering with the person's work performance or has the purpose or effect of creating an intimidating, hostile, or offensive working environment. Harassing conduct includes but is not limited to epithets, slurs or negative stereotyping, threatening, intimidating, or hostile acts, denigrating jokes and display or circulation in the workplace of written or graphic material that denigrates or shows hostility or aversion toward an individual or group based on their protected characteristic.

Sexual harassment is defined as unwelcome sexual advances, requests for sexual favors, and other verbal, visual, or physical conduct of a sexual nature when:

1. Submission to such conduct is made either explicitly or implicitly a term or condition of an individual's employment;
2. Submission to or rejection of such conduct by an individual is used as the basis for employment decisions affecting such individual; or
3. Such conduct has the purpose or effect of unreasonably interfering with an individual's work performance or creating an intimidating, hostile, or offensive working environment.

Examples of sexual harassment include unwelcome or unsolicited sexual advances; displaying sexually suggestive material; unwelcome sexual flirtations, advances or propositions; suggestive comments; verbal abuse of a sexual nature; sexually oriented jokes; crude or vulgar language or gestures; graphic or verbal commentaries about an individual's body; display or distribution of obscene materials; physical contact such as patting, pinching or brushing against someone's body; or physical assault of a sexual nature.

Reporting: any company employee who feels that he or she has been harassed or discriminated against or has witnessed or become aware of discrimination or harassment in violation of these policies should bring the matter to the immediate attention of his or her supervisor or [enter name of alternative person to whom employees can report]. The company will promptly investigate all allegations of discrimination and harassment and take action as appropriate based on the outcome of the investigation. An investigation and its results will be treated as confidential to the extent feasible, and the company will take appropriate action based on the outcome of the investigation.

No employee will be retaliated against for making a complaint in good faith regarding a violation of these policies or for participating in good faith in an investigation pursuant to these policies. If an employee feels he/she has been retaliated against, the employee should file a complaint using the procedures set forth above.

It is important for employers to implement nonharassment policies, including a provision regarding reporting procedures. To the extent that an employee fails to report harassment by a coemployee as required by an established policy, this may be a possible defense in response to a legal action initiated by the employee. Once in place, the company should make sure that the policy is carried out, including prompt investigation of claims of discrimination and harassment.

2.3 Drug-free/Alcohol-free environment

Employees are prohibited from unlawfully consuming, distributing, possessing, selling, or using controlled substances while on duty. In addition, employees may not be under the influence of any controlled substance, such as drugs or alcohol, while at work, on company premises, or engaged in company business. Prescription drugs or over-the-counter medications, taken as prescribed, are an exception to this policy.

Anyone violating this policy may be subject to disciplinary action, up to and including termination.

2.4 Open-door policy

The company has an open-door policy and takes employee concerns and problems seriously. The company values each employee and strives to provide a positive work experience. Employees are encouraged to bring any workplace concerns or problems they might have or know about to their supervisor or some other member of management.

SECTION 3

Company Policies and Procedures

3.1 Professional conduct

This company expects its employees to adhere to a standard of professional conduct and integrity. This ensures that the work environment is safe, comfortable, and productive. Employees should be respectful, courteous, and mindful of others' feelings and needs. General cooperation between coworkers and supervisors is expected. Individuals who act in an unprofessional manner may be subject to disciplinary action.

3.2 Dress code

An employee's personal appearance and hygiene is a reflection on the company's character. Employees are expected to dress appropriately for their individual work responsibilities and position.

3.3 Payday

Paychecks are distributed every [dates] after [time]. If the pay date lands on a holiday, paychecks will be distributed on the closest business day before the holiday.

The paycheck will reflect work performed for the [enter pay period dates, commission period dates, etc.] period. Paychecks include salary or wages earned less any mandatory or elected deductions. Mandatory deductions include federal or state withholding tax and other withholdings. Elected deductions are deductions authorized by the employee, and may include, for example, contributions to benefit plans. Employees may contact [enter authorized person's name] to obtain the necessary authorization forms for requesting additional deductions from their paychecks.

Notify a supervisor if the paycheck appears to be inaccurate or if it has been misplaced. The company reserves the right to charge a replacement fee for any lost paychecks. Advances on paychecks [are/are not] permitted. Information regarding final paychecks can be found under the termination section of this handbook.

This section may be expanded to include the specific requirements of your company. Include information regarding uniforms, safety protections, such as steel toe shoes or hairnets or other dress requirements. If the company provides uniforms, consider including a caveat about lost uniform charges or laundry.

Any change in name, address, telephone number, marital status, or number of exemptions claimed by an employee must be reported to [enter authorized person's name] immediately.

3.4 Company property

Company property, such as equipment, vehicles, telephones, computers, and software, is not for private use. These devices are to be used strictly for company business and are not permitted off grounds unless authorized. Company property must be used in the manner for which it was intended. Upon termination, employees are required to surrender any company property they possess.

Company computers, Internet, and emails are a privileged resource and must be used only to complete essential job-related functions. Employees are not permitted to download any "pirated" software, files, or programs and must receive permission from a supervisor before installing any new software on a company computer. Files or programs stored on company computers may not be copied for personal use.

Phones are provided for business use. The company requests that employees not receive personal calls while on duty. If urgent, please keep personal calls to a minimum and conversations brief. Personal long-distance calls are not permitted.

Employees are reminded that they should have no expectation of privacy in their use of company computers or other electronic equipment.

Violations of these policies could result in disciplinary action.

Companies should consult state and local law for wage payment requirements, such as means of payment (including opportunity to pay by direct deposit), timeframe for paying wages, and information that must be included on paycheck stubs.

Companies may institute a policy of "business use only." Alternatively, a company may adopt a less stringent policy which advises employees that computers and phones are provided for business use, and any personal use must be kept to a minimum and must not interfere with work responsibilities. Companies should develop a policy specific to their own computer systems that protects against employee misuse and the computer viruses that may result from downloading outside materials.

3.5 Privacy

Employees and employers share a relationship based on trust and mutual respect. However, the company retains the right to access all company property including computers, desks, file cabinets, storage facilities, and files and folders, electronic or otherwise, at any time. Employees should not entertain any expectations of privacy when on company grounds or while using company property.

All documents, files, voice mails, and electronic information, including e-mails and other communications, created, received, or maintained on or through company property are the property of the company, not the employee. Therefore, employees should have no expectation of privacy over those files or documents.

3.6 Personnel Files

The company maintains a personnel file on each employee. These files are kept confidential to the extent possible. Employees may review their personnel file upon request.

It is important that personnel files accurately reflect each employee's personal information. Employees are expected to inform the company of any change in name, address, home phone number, home address, marital status, number of dependents, or emergency contact information.

If you plan to enforce a privacy policy, ensure that you are very explicit about what the company expects. Privacy laws are relatively new and vary from state to state. Consult with an employment attorney regarding your state's privacy laws.

Employers should consult state and local law regarding any provisions relating to employee access to personnel files. In the absence of such a provision, the company may not be required to allow employees to have access to their personnel files. However, the company may nonetheless allow employees to have access. In the event that a company allows employee access, the company may want to consider limiting the access to by appointment only during normal business hours.

SECTION 4

Employment Classification

This company assigns positions, determines wages, and compensates employees for overtime in accordance with state and local laws and the Fair Labor Standards Act.

4.1 Exempt employees

Exempt employees are those that are excluded from the overtime pay requirements of the Fair Labor Standards Act. Exempt employees are paid a salary and are expected to work beyond their normal work hours whenever necessary to accomplish the work of the company. Exempt employees are not eligible to receive overtime compensation. Employees should consult with an administrator if they have questions regarding their classification as an exempt employee.

4.2 Nonexempt employees

Nonexempt employees are those eligible for overtime pay of 1.5 times the regular hourly rate of pay for all hours worked over 40 per workweek. All overtime must be approved in advance. Employees should consult with an administrator if they have questions regarding their classification as a nonexempt employee.

The Fair Labor Standards Act provides narrow provisions for who qualifies for exempt employee status. Consult the Department of Labor's website at http://www.dol.gov/esa/regs/ compliance/whd/ hrg.htm#2 for more information.

The Fair Labor Standards Act limits the employers that must pay overtime wages to employees to those engaged in "interstate commerce" and other particular types of businesses. Companies should consult an attorney if there is a question about an obligation to pay overtime wages. Companies should also consult state and local law regarding broader overtime coverage than is provided under the federal Fair Labor Standards Act. For example, some jurisdictions may require companies to pay overtime for all hours work in a day over 8 hours rather than using the federal standard of paying overtime for all hours worked over 40 hours in a given workweek.

4.3   Part-time, full-time or temporary status

Part-time or full-time status depends on the number of hours per week an employee works. Regular employees who work fewer than [enter hours] receive part-time classification. Part-time employees [are/are not] eligible for employee benefits as described in this handbook. Regular employees who work at least [enter hours] receive full-time classification.

From time to time, the company may hire employees for specific projects or periods of time. Temporary employees may work either part-time or full-time but generally are scheduled to terminate by a certain date. Temporary employees who remain on duty past the scheduled termination remain classified as temporary. Only [enter authorized person's name] may change an employee's temporary status. Temporary employees are not eligible for employment benefits.

SECTION 5

Attendance Policies

5.1 General attendance

The company maintains normal working hours of [enter hours]. Hours may vary depending on work location and job responsibilities. Supervisors will provide employees with their work schedule. Should an employee have any questions regarding his/her work schedule, the employee should contact the supervisor.

The company does not tolerate absenteeism without excuse. Employees who will be late to or absent from work should notify a supervisor in advance, or as soon as practicable in the event of an emergency. Chronic absenteeism may result in disciplinary action.

Employees who need to leave early, for illness or otherwise, should inform a supervisor before departure. Unauthorized departures may result in disciplinary action.

5.2 Tardiness

Employees are expected to arrive on time and ready for work. An employee who arrives [enter time period] after their scheduled arrival time is considered tardy. The company recognizes that situations arise which hinder punctuality; regardless, excessive tardiness is prohibited and may be subject to disciplinary action.

5.3 Breaks

When working conditions permit, and pending a supervisor's approval, employees are entitled to [enter number] [enter time] minute breaks for every [enter hours] hours worked.

Meal periods are for [enter time] minutes and must be approved by a supervisor.

The laws regarding break and meal periods are different for each state. Consult with an employment attorney regarding your state's laws.

SECTION 6

Leave Policies

6.1 Vacations

The company provides, as a benefit, paid vacations for its eligible employees. Forward requests for time off in advance to a supervisor, who may approve or deny the request based on company resources. The company is flexible in approving time off when doing so would not interfere with company operations. Vacation days are granted only on a full-day or half-day basis.

A regular employee is eligible to receive paid time off after [enter number] months of full-time service. Accrued time off may be taken after [enter eligibility dates]. Employees must earn and accrue vacation benefits before they may be used. Employees should consult [enter authorized person's name] regarding the amount of vacation leave they accrue each pay period.

Any remaining accrued time off [may/may not] be accumulated or carried forward into the next year. Vacation benefits [do/do not] accrue during any period of extended leave of absence.

6.2 Sick leave

Situations may arise where an employee needs to take time off to address medical or other health concerns. The company requests that employees provide notification to their supervisor as soon as practicable when taking time off. Sick days are granted on a [paid/unpaid] basis to regular employees. Employees may consult [enter authorized person's name] regarding the amount of (paid) sick leave provided each year. Sick days may not be carried over into the next year. Abuse of this policy may result in disciplinary action.

6.3 Family and Medical Leave Act leave

The company offers leave consistent with the requirements of the federal Family and Medical Leave Act (FMLA). Under the FMLA, an employee may be eligible for an

Generally, states do not require vacation benefits for employees, but most employers offer this benefit. If you have a set vacation accrual for your company, insert it into this section. Replace this section if your company provides paid time off instead of vacation and sick leave.

Unpaid family and medical leave of absence under certain circumstances, if the employee works within a seventy-five (75) mile radius of fifty (50) or more company employees.

Under the federal FMLA, a person who has worked as an employee of this company for at least 1,250 hours for twelve months is eligible for FMLA leave. Up to twelve weeks of unpaid leave per year is available for the following reasons:

- The birth of a child and to care for the newborn child;
- Placement of a child into adoptive or foster care with the employee;
- Care for a spouse, son, daughter, or parent who has a serious health condition; or
- Care for the employee's own serious health condition.

If the need for leave is foreseeable, employees should notify a supervisor 30 days prior to taking FMLA leave. If the need for FMLA leave arises unexpectedly, employees should notify a supervisor as soon as practicable, giving as much notice to the company as possible. Employees may be required to provide medical certifications supporting the need for leave if the leave is due to a serious health condition of the employee or employee's family member; periodic recertification of the serious health condition; and periodic reports during the leave regarding the employee's status and intent to return to work. Employees must return to work immediately after the serious health condition ceases, and employees who have taken leave because of their own serious health condition must submit a fitness-for-duty certification before being allowed to return to work. Leave may be taken on an intermittent or reduced schedule to care for an illness yet may not be taken intermittently for the care of a newborn or newly adopted child. When leave is taken intermittently, the company may transfer the employee to another position with equivalent pay and benefits, which is better suited to periods of absence. Subject to certain conditions, the employee or the company may choose to use accrued paid leave (such as sick leave or vacation leave) concurrent with FMLA leave. The company will maintain group health insurance coverage for an employee on family and medical leave on the same terms as if the employee had continued work. If applicable, arrangements will be made for the employee to pay their share of health insurance premiums while on leave. The company may recover premiums paid to maintain health coverage for an employee who fails to return to work from family and medical leave.

If an employee would like the company to maintain other paid benefits during the period of leave, premiums and charges which are partially or wholly paid by the employee must continue to be paid by the employee during the leave time.

Family and medical leave will not result in the loss of any employment benefit accrued prior to the date on which the leave commenced. However, an employee on family and medical leave does not continue to accrue benefits (e.g., sick leave or vacation leave) during the period of family and medical leave. Questions regarding particular benefits should be directed to [enter authorized person's name].

Upon returning from FMLA leave, an employee will be restored to his/her original job or an equivalent job with equivalent benefits, pay, seniority, and other employment terms and conditions as provided by the Family and Medical Leave Act.

If your company has 50 or more employees, you are required to comply with the Family and Medical Leave Act. If you are covered, your manual should include a FMLA section. For more information on the FMLA, visit the Department of Labor's website at www.dol.gov/esa/whd/fmla/index.htm. In addition, some states and local jurisdictions, including the District of Columbia, provide broader family and medical leave coverage to employees, so you should consult an attorney regarding applicable state and local laws. If your company is required to comply with the FMLA, you may consider requiring employees to exhaust their accrued paid leave at the same time they are on FMLA leave. Otherwise, an employee could take up to 12 weeks of FMLA leave in addition to all of his/her accrued vacation and sick leave.

6.4 Holidays

The company observes the following holidays:

- New Year's Day
- Martin Luther King Day
- Memorial Day
- Independence Day
- Labor Day
- Thanksgiving (2 Days)

- Birthday
- Voted on floater day
- Christmas Day
- [list other observed holidays]

Holidays are observed on a [paid/unpaid] basis for all eligible employees. [Full time employees are eligible for paid holiday benefits.]

Companies should consult state and local law to determine if there are any mandated holidays in the jurisdictions in which they are located.

6.5 Jury duty time off

The company understands that occasionally employees are called to serve on a jury. Employees who are selected for jury duty must provide a copy of their jury summons to a supervisor. Time taken for jury duty is granted on a [paid/unpaid] basis. Employees released from jury duty with [enter number] hours remaining in the workday are expected to return to work.

6.6 Voting time off

Employees are encouraged to participate in elections. The company grants incremental time off to cast a ballot in an election. Voting time off is granted on a [paid/unpaid] basis. Should extenuating circumstances arise while voting, notify a supervisor as soon as possible.

6.7 Military leave

Employees called to active military duty, military reserve, or National Guard service may be eligible to receive time off under the Uniformed Services Employment and Reemployment Rights Act of 1994. To receive time off, employees must provide notice and a copy of their report orders to an immediate supervisor. Military leave is granted on a [paid/unpaid] basis [if leave is on a paid basis, indicate the maximum number of days of paid leave to be provided by the company]. Upon return with an honorable discharge, an employee may be entitled to reinstatement and any applicable job benefits they would have received if present, to the extent provided by law.

Most state laws prohibit an employer from taking any disciplinary action against employees for taking time off to vote or serve on a jury. Some states even require the time off to be granted on a paid basis. If your state requires paid jury/voting time off, be sure to provide as much detail as possible about your leave provisions.

Every company, regardless of the number of people employed, is required to comply with the Uniformed Services Employment and Reemployment Rights Act. Under the act, employers are prevented from taking disciplinary action against an employee because of their military status. For more information on the USERRA, visit the Department of Labor's website at http://www.dol.gov/elaws/vets/userra/mainmenu.asp.

6.8 Leave of absence

Regular full-time employees may request an unpaid leave of absence after the exhaustion of paid leave. A request for a leave of absence must be submitted in writing in advance to the employee's immediate supervisor.

Leave of absences that are granted are unpaid and will not be considered until an employee has exhausted all appropriate accrued leave balances. Continuation of employee benefits during a leave of absence will be addressed on an individual basis, as required by law.

Companies should consider establishing a leave of absence policy. It is a common practice for companies to consider employees' requests for unpaid leaves of absence. In particular, it may be appropriate for a company to allow a qualified disabled employee to take additional unpaid leave beyond the amount of leave he/she may be entitled to under the Family and Medical Leave Act. As a result, it may make sense to provide employees with a written policy on this benefit.

SECTION 7

Work Performance

7.1 Expectations

The company expects every employee to act in a professional manner. Satisfactory performance of job duties and responsibilities is key to this expectation. Employees should attempt to achieve their job objectives, and act with diligence and consideration at all times. Poor job performance can result in disciplinary action, up to and including termination.

7.2 Reviews

The company may periodically evaluate an employee's performance. The goal of a performance review is to identify areas where an employee excels and areas that need improvement. The company uses performance reviews as a tool to determine pay increases, promotions, and/or terminations.

All performance reviews are based on merit, achievement, and other factors may include but are not limited to the following:

- Quality of work
- Attitude
- Knowledge of work
- Job skills

- Attendance and punctuality
- Teamwork and cooperation
- Compliance with company policy
- Past performance reviews
- Improvement
- Acceptance of responsibility and constructive feedback

Employees should note that a performance review does not guarantee a pay increase or promotion. Written performance evaluations may be made at any time to advise employees of unacceptable performance. Evaluations or any subsequent change in employment status, position, or pay does not alter the employee's at-will relationship with the company. Forward any questions about performance expectation or evaluation to the supervisor conducting the evaluation.

Companies that adhere to a performance review policy can avoid problems handling "poor performance" terminations. If your company has a review policy, it is not necessary to include the whole policy in the handbook. Adding a simple timeline of when employees may expect a review is sufficient.

7.3 Insubordination

Supervisors and employees should interact with mutual respect and common courtesy. Employees are expected to take instruction from supervisors or other persons of authority. Failure to comply with instructions or unreasonably delaying compliance is considered insubordination. Acts of insubordination are subject to disciplinary action, up to and including termination.

If an employee disagrees with a supervisor, the employee should first try to mediate the situation by explaining their position. If possible, a compromise might be met and accusations of insubordination avoided.

SECTION 8

Discipline Policy

8.1 Grounds for disciplinary action

The company reserves the right to discipline and/or terminate any employee who violates company polices, practices, or rules of conduct. Poor performance and misconduct are also grounds for discipline or termination.

The following actions are unacceptable and considered grounds for disciplinary action. This list is not comprehensive; rather, it is meant merely as an example of the types of conduct that this company does not tolerate. These actions include, but are not limited to the following:

- Engaging in acts of discrimination or harassment in the workplace;
- Possessing, distributing, or being under the influence of illicit controlled substances;
- Being under the influence of a controlled substance or alcohol at work, on company premises, or while engaged in company business;
- Unauthorized use of company property, equipment, devices, or assets;
- Damage, destruction, or theft of company property, equipment, devices, or assets;

- Removing company property without prior authorization or disseminating company information without authorization;
- Falsification, misrepresentation or omission of information, documents, or records;
- Lying;
- Insubordination or refusal to comply with directives;
- Failing to adequately perform job responsibilities;
- Excessive or unexcused absenteeism or tardiness;
- Disclosing confidential or proprietary company information without permission;
- Illegal or violent activity;
- Falsifying injury reports or reasons for leave;
- Possessing unauthorized weapons on premises;
- Disregard for safety and security procedures;
- Disparaging or disrespecting supervisors and/or coworkers; and
- Any other action or conduct that is inconsistent with company policies, procedures, standards, or expectations. This list exhibits the types of actions or events that are subject to disciplinary action. It is not intended to indicate every act that could lead to disciplinary action. The company reserves the right to determine the severity and extent of any disciplinary action based on the circumstances of each case.

8.2 Procedures

Disciplinary action is any one of a number of options used to correct unacceptable behavior or actions. Discipline may take the form of oral warnings, written warnings, probation, suspension, demotion, discharge, removal, or some other disciplinary action, in no particular order. The course of action will be determined by the company at its sole discretion as it deems appropriate.

If your company uses a progressive discipline system, placing that policy in a handbook can be binding. You are guarantying to your employees that the company follows a set method for discipline each and every time. Companies could become liable for not adhering to their own policies in every situation. In addition, progressive discipline polices can sometimes defeat the purposes of an at-will employment relationship.

When drafting your discipline section, do not over explain the policy or include steps that you might not take every time. If you do plan to include a progressive discipline policy in your handbook, have an employment attorney review your submission.

8.3 Termination

Employment with the company is on an at-will basis and may be terminated voluntarily or involuntarily at any time.

Upon termination, an employee is required:

- To continue to work until the last scheduled day of employment;
- To turn in all reports and paperwork required to be completed by the employee when due and no later than the last day of work;
- To return all files, documents, equipment, keys, access cards, software, or other property belonging to the com-

pany that are in the employee's possession, custody, or control, and turn in all passwords to his/her supervisor;

- To participate in an exit interview as requested by [enter authorized person's name].

SECTION 9

Health and Safety

9.1 Workplace safety

The company takes every reasonable precaution to ensure that employees have a safe, working environment. Safety measures and rules are in place for the protection of all employees. Ultimately, it is the responsibility of each employee to help prevent accidents. To ensure the continuation of a safe workplace, all employees should review and understand all provisions of the company's workplace safety policy. Employees should use all safety and protective equipment provided to them and maintain work areas in a safe and orderly manner, free from hazardous conditions. Employees who observe an unsafe practice or condition should report it to a supervisor or [enter alternate name] immediately. Employees are prohibited from making threats against anyone in connection with his/her work or engaging in violent activities while in the employ of the company. Any questions regarding safety and safe practices should be directed to [enter authorized person's name].

In the event of an accident, employees must notify a supervisor immediately. Report every injury, regardless of how minor, to a supervisor immediately. Physical discomfort caused by repetitive tasks must also be reported. For more information about on-the-job injuries, refer to the worker's compensation section of this handbook.

Employees should recognize any potential fire hazards and be aware of fire escape routes and fire drills. Do not block fire exits, tamper with fire extinguishers, or otherwise create fire hazards.

9.2 Workplace security

Employees must be alert and aware of any potential dangers to themselves or their coworkers. Take every precaution to ensure that your surroundings are safe and secure. Guard personal belongings and company property. Visitors should be escorted at all times. Report any suspicious activity to a supervisor immediately.

9.3 Emergency procedures

In the event of an emergency, dial 911 immediately. If you hear a fire alarm or other emergency alert system, proceed quickly and calmly to the nearest exit. Once the building has been evacuated, only a supervisor may authorize employees to reenter.

Expand this section to include any industry-specific safety guidelines your company must follow, such as OSHA standards and regulations. Include the name of the accident contact person and the location of safety posters that your company is required to post. If you are in a highly regulated industry, consider providing a separate employee safety manual. If you have company vehicles, include a section on accident reporting.

SECTION 10

Employee Benefits

This handbook contains descriptions of some of our current employee benefits. Many of the company's benefit plans are described in more formal plan documents available from [enter authorized person's name]. In the event of any inconsistencies between this handbook or any other oral or written description of benefits and a formal plan document, the formal plan document will govern.

10.1 Health insurance

The company makes group health benefits available to eligible employees and their family members. Eligible employees are full time employees who have worked for [enter time] months. Part time employees are eligible if they work at least [enter hours] hours per week and have been employed for [enter time] months.

Health benefits are paid in part by the company. The remainder of the costs is the employee's responsibility. Employees can receive details about benefits provided, contribution rates, and eligibility from [enter authorized person's name].

10.2 Retirement plan

The company participates in a 401(k) or SIMPLE IRA plan so that employees may save a portion of their earnings for retirement.

Regular employees who have worked at least [enter hours] for [enter months] are eligible to participate. Employees may elect to make regular contributions to the 401(k) plan up to the maximum amount allowed by federal law.

Contact [enter authorized person's name] for detailed information regarding eligibility, employee contributions, vesting period, or employer contributions. More information can also be found in the plan summary description, which is available from [enter benefits coordinator name]. If there are any inconsistencies between this handbook and any of the Summary Plan Descriptions, the Summary Plan Descriptions shall govern. The company reserves the right to modify or terminate any or all of its retirement benefits or to change benefit providers at any time with or without notice.

Even with the disclaimer language provided above, it is important to conform the benefit plans described in the handbook with the company's formal plan documents. It is not necessary to provide detailed information about the benefit plans in the handbook, but it may be helpful to provide general information on the types of benefits provided and where employees can find more detailed information on the benefits provided.

This section should briefly describe the company's offered benefits. A detailed account of the plan's characteristics is not necessary. Simply include a basic description of the benefits offered, the eligibility requirements, and a contact name. To provide more information about a specific plan, create a benefits handbook or ask the plan administrator for an informational booklet to present to eligible employees.

10.3 Workers' compensation

As required by law, the company provides workers' compensation benefits for the protection of employees with work-related injuries or illnesses.

Workers' compensation insurance provides coverage to employees who receive job-related injuries or illnesses. If an employee is injured or becomes ill as a result of his/her job, it is the employee's responsibility to immediately notify a supervisor of their injury in order to receive benefits. Report every illness or injury to a supervisor, regardless of how minor it appears. The company will advise the employee of the procedure for submitting a workers' compensation claim. If necessary, injured employees will be referred to a medical care facility. Employees should retain all paperwork provided to them by the medical facility. Failure to report a work-related illness or injury promptly could result in denial of benefits. An employee's report should contain as many details as possible, including the date, time, description of the illness or injury, and the names of any witnesses.

A separate insurance company administers the worker's compensation insurance. Representatives of this company may contact injured employees regarding their benefits under the plan. Additional information regarding workers' compensation is available from [enter authorized person's name].

10.4 Disability coverage

Disability insurance provides partial paycheck reimbursement for times of serious illness or injury which leads to total disability. Total disability is defined as the inability to perform any job function as a result of the injury or illness. Employees who have worked for [enter number] months are eligible for disability insurance coverage. To qualify for benefits, the period of total disability must exceed [enter number] days.

Worker's compensation can be required, and the laws vary from state to state. Check with your state worker's compensation agency to determine if you are required to carry worker's compensation insurance.

Coverage extends for [enter number] days of disability. Employees must exhaust any sick leave benefits before being eligible for disability leave coverage.

Disability benefits are calculated as [enter percentage] of an employee's base salary. Any payments received from worker's compensation or state disability will result in an equal decrease in disability benefits. Disability benefits are subject to employment-withholding provisions.

The employee is responsible for notifying a supervisor of their disability, expected date of return, and the name of their attending physician. The company may request that an independent medical provider perform an examination. In addition, the company may require a medical release form prior to returning to work. For more information regarding disability benefits, contact [enter authorized person's name]. If there are any inconsistencies between this handbook and any of the Summary Plan Descriptions, the Summary Plan Descriptions shall govern. The company reserves the right to modify or terminate any or all of the benefits or to change benefit providers at any time with or without notice.

Disability insurance is generally not required; but if your company provides disability benefits, include a brief description in your handbook.

Companies with more than 15 employees are required to comply with the Americans with Disabilities Act. For more information about the ADA, visit the ADA home page at http://www.usdoj.gov/crt/ada/adahom1.htm.

SECTION 11

Termination

11.1 Voluntary termination

The company recognizes that personal situations may arise which require a voluntary termination of employment. Should this occur, the company requests that the employee provide two weeks advance notice in writing. This request does not alter an employee's at-will relationship with the company.

All rights and privileges of employment with the company terminate upon the date of separation. As further discussed in section 8.3, terminating employees are required to return all company property assigned to them. Failure to do so may result in the withholding of their final paycheck.

11.2 Final paycheck

Employees who terminate employment with the company will be given their final pay check [enter time required by state law]. Should the employee be unable to personally retrieve their paycheck, it will be mailed to the address on file.

11.3 COBRA continuation of health benefits

Under the federal Consolidated Omnibus Budget Reconciliation Act (COBRA), a qualified employee who terminates employment (for reasons other than gross misconduct on the employee's part) or who loses health and dental coverage due to a reduction in work hours may temporarily continue group health and dental coverage for himself/herself, his/her spouse, and any covered dependent children at the full premium rate plus administrative fees. That eligibility normally extends for a period of eighteen (18) months from the qualifying date. For more information regarding COBRA health insurance benefits, see [enter authorized person's name].

Most states require that a terminated employee receive their paycheck within a certain number of days after termination. Consult with an employment attorney to determine what your state requires.

11.4 Exit interview

The company may request an exit interview upon notice of termination. The purpose of the exit interview is to complete necessary forms, collect company property, and discuss employment experiences with the company.

ACKNOWLEDGMENT OF RECEIPT FOR EMPLOYEE HANDBOOK

(Employee Copy, Keep with Handbook)

I acknowledge that I have received a copy of the employee handbook. I understand that I am responsible for reading the information contained in the handbook.

I understand that the handbook is intended to provide me with a general overview of the company's policies and procedures. I acknowledge that nothing in this handbook is to be interpreted as a contract, expressed or implied, or an inducement for employment, nor does it guarantee my employment for any period of time.

I understand and accept that my employment with the company is at will. I have the right to resign at any time with or without cause, just as the company may terminate my employment at any time with or without cause or notice, subject to applicable laws. I understand that nothing in the handbook or in any oral or written statement alters the at-will relationship, except by written agreement signed by the employee and [enter authorized person's name].

I acknowledge that the company may revise, suspend, revoke, terminate, change, or remove, prospectively or retroactively, any of the policies or procedures outlined in this handbook or elsewhere, in whole or in part, with or without notice at any time, at the company's sole discretion.

_____ (Signature of Employee)
_____ (Date)
_____ (Company Representative)
_____   _____

Acknowledgement of Receipt for Employee Handbook (Employer Copy—detach and retain for records) I acknowledge that I have received a copy of the employee handbook. I understand that I am responsible for reading the information contained in the handbook.

I understand that the handbook is intended to provide me with a general overview of the company's policies and procedures. I acknowledge that nothing in this handbook is to be interpreted as a contract, expressed or implied, or an inducement for employment, nor does it guarantee my employment for any period of time.

I understand and accept that my employment with the company is at will. I have the right to resign at any time with or without cause, just as the company may terminate my employment at any time with or without cause or notice, subject to applicable laws. I understand that nothing in the handbook or in any oral or written statement alters the at-will relationship, except by written agreement signed by the employee and [enter authorized person's name].

I acknowledge that the company may revise, suspend, revoke, terminate, change, or remove, prospectively or retroactively, any of the policies or procedures of the company, whether outlined in this handbook or elsewhere, in whole or in part, with or without notice at any time, at the company's sole discretion.

_____ (Signature of Employee)

_____ (Date)

_____ (Company Representative)

Companies may also consider instituting some of the following policies, depending on the nature of the company's business and workforce:

- Confidentiality
- Conflict of interest

- Intellectual property ownership
- Outside employment
- Additional benefits, such as training or education reimbursement
- Expense reporting
- Use of company vehicles

EMPLOYEE FORMS AND DOCUMENTS

1) Employee Intellectual Property Agreement
2) Team Member Checklist
3) Employee Information Record
4) Job Performance and Evaluation Form
5) Time Sheet

Employee Intellectual Property and Confidentiality Agreement

In consideration of my employment in any capacity with [company name and address] [type of company, i.e., LLC], or any of its subsidiaries (collectively, the "company") and with respect to my providing services to any of the company's affiliates (as hereinafter defined), and in consideration of the salary, wages, benefits, and/or compensation paid for my services in the course of such employment by the company, I agree as follows:

1) All inventions, writings, software, source codes, databases, trademarks, service marks, product concepts, marketing plans, prototypes, discoveries, developments, improvements, modifications, and innovations (hereinafter referred to as "inventions") shall be the exclusive property of the company and its affiliates whether patentable/copyrightable or not, conceived by me or not, either solely or in conjunction with others, during the period of my employment with the company, including, but not limited to, any period subsequent to the commencement of my employ-

ment, whether or not made or conceived during work hours which, (1) relate in any manner to the existing or contemplated business or research activities of the company and its affiliates, or its customers; or (2) result from the use, in any way, of the time, material, equipment, software, documentation, records, or facilities of the company and its affiliates or its customers.

2) I agree that I shall promptly and fully disclose to the company, in writing, all such inventions, regardless of the stage of development or completion, and I agree to keep and maintain adequate and current written records of all such inventions, which records shall be and remain the property of and available to the company and its affiliates.

3) I hereby assign to the company or its affiliates, as the case may be, without further compensation, my entire right, title and interest to all such inventions, which are the property of the company or its affiliates under the foregoing provisions of this agreement.

4) I agree that an invention disclosed by me to a third party or described in a patent or copyright application filed by me on my behalf within six months following the period of my employment with the company shall be presumed to have been conceived or made by me during the period of my employment and thus shall be presumed to be the exclusive property of the company or its affiliates, unless (1) proved by me to have been conceived and made by me following the termination of my employment, or (2) proved by me to be not directly or indirectly related in any manner to the business, intellectual properties, and technologies of the company or its affiliates.

5) I will not, during the term of my employment with the company or twelve (12) months after the termination of my employment, use for myself or others or divulge or convey to others any confidential information as hereinafter described (the "information"). "Information" means all marketing information, customer lists, sales and mar-

ket data, product literature, product information, product specifications, bills of material, engineering drawings, personnel information, organizational data, financial data, engineering designs, software code, software documentation, contracts, research and development activities, including any records, reports, or other documents obtained by me, about the company and its affiliates. Information shall not include, however, information which (a) is or becomes publicly available or (b) is or becomes available to me on a nonconfidential basis from a source which, to the best of that party's knowledge, is not prohibited from disclosing such information to me by a legal, contractual, or fiduciary obligation.

6) I further agree to (a) keep the information confidential and will not (except as required by applicable law or regulation), without the company's or the affiliate's prior written consent, disclose any information in any manner whatsoever, and (b) not use any of the information for any purpose other than in carrying out the duties of my employment, provided, however, that I may reveal the information to applicable customers, vendors, suppliers, employees, advisors, and representatives, who need to have knowledge of such information for the sole purpose of carrying out the duties of my employment. In the event I am requested pursuant to any applicable law or regulation to disclose any of the information, I agree to contact the company immediately in writing, stating the nature and details of the request for the information.

7) Upon termination of my employment with the company, or at any time at the company's request, I agree to promptly deliver any information and all copies thereof to the company.

8) The invalidity or unenforceability of any provision of this agreement, as applied to a particular occurrence or circumstance or otherwise, shall not affect the validity or

enforceability or applicability of any other provision of this agreement.

9) This agreement shall inure to the benefit of and may be enforced by the company and its affiliates, their respective successors or assigns, and shall be binding upon me, my executors, administrators, legatees, and other successors in interest and may not be changed in whole or in part except in writing signed by an authorized representative of the company and myself.

10) The internal substantive laws of the State of Ohio shall govern this agreement.

11) With respect to the subject matter hereof, this agreement comprises the entire agreement among the parties and, as of the last signature date below (the effective date), supersedes, cancels, and annuls all previous agreements between the company and me (whether written or oral). The terms of this agreement are intended by the parties to be the final expression of their agreement with respect to the subject matter hereof and may not be contradicted by evidence of any prior or contemporaneous agreement, whether written or oral.

12) This Agreement may only be amended or modified by a written instrument signed by all parties.

Accepted and agreed to as of the date below:

[Company Name]

By _____ Signed _____
Name _____ Name _____
Date_____ Date _____

Company
LOGO

Team Member Checklist

Employee Information	
Name:	Start date:
Position:	Manager:

First Day

☐ Provide employee with New Employee Workbook.
☐ Assign "buddy" employee(s) to answer general questions.

Policies

☐ Review key policies.	• Anti-harassment • Vacation and sick leave • FMLA/leaves of absence • Holidays • Time and leave reporting • Overtime • Performance reviews • Dress code	• Personal conduct standards • Progressive disciplinary actions • Security • Confidentiality • Safety • Emergency procedures • Visitors • E-mail and Internet use

Administrative procedures

☐ Review general administrative procedures.	• Office/desk/work station • Keys • Mail (incoming and outgoing) • Shipping (FedEx, DHL, and UPS) • Business cards • Purchase requests	• Telephones • Building access cards • Conference rooms • Picture ID badges • Expense reports • Office supplies

Introductions and Tours			
☐ Give introductions to department staff and key personnel during tour.			
☐ Tour of facility, including:	• Restrooms • Mail rooms • Copy centers • Fax machines	• Bulletin board • Parking • Printers • Office supplies	• Kitchen • Coffee/vending machines • Cafeteria • Emergency exits and supplies
Position Information			
☐ Introductions to team. ☐ Review initial job assignments and training plans. ☐ Review job description and performance expectations and standards. ☐ Review job schedule and hours. ☐ Review payroll timing, time cards (if applicable), and policies and procedures.			
Computers			
☐ Hardware and software reviews, including:	• E-mail • Internet	• Microsoft Office system • Data on shared drives	• Databases • Internet

Company LOGO

Employee Information

Personal Information		

Full Name: _____
Last .... *First* .... *M.I.*

Address: _____
Street Address .... *Apartment/Unit #*

_____
City .... *State* .... *ZIP Code*

Home Phone: ( ) _____ Alternate Phone: ( ) _____

E-mail Address: _____

Social Security Number or Government ID: _____

Birth Date: _____ Marital Status: _____

Spouse's Name: _____

Spouse's Employer: _____ Spouse's Work Phone: ( ) _____

Job Information	

Title: _____ Employee ID: _____

Supervisor: _____ Department: _____

Work Location: _____ E-mail Address: _____

Work Phone: ( ) _____ Cell Phone: ( ) _____

Start Date: _____ Salary: $ _____

Emergency Contact Information		

Full Name: _____
Last .... *First* .... *M.I.*

Address: _____
Street Address .... *Apartment/Unit #*

_____
City .... *State* .... *ZIP Code*

Primary Phone: ( ) _____ Alternate Phone: ( ) _____

Relationship: _____

Job Performance Evaluation Form

Name:

Evaluation Period:

Title: Date:

Performance Planning and Results

Performance review

- Use a current job description (job descriptions are available on the HR web page).
- Rate the person's level of performance, using the definitions below.
- Review with employee each performance factor used to evaluate his/her work performance.
- Give an overall rating in the space provided, using the definitions below as a guide.

Performance rating definitions

The following ratings must be used to ensure commonality of language and consistency on overall ratings. (There should be supporting comments to justify ratings of "Outstanding," "Below Expectations, and "Unsatisfactory.")

Outstanding	Performance is consistently superior.
Exceeds Expectations	Performance is routinely above-job requirements.
Meets Expectations	Performance is regularly competent and dependable.
Below Expectations	Performance fails to meet job requirements on a frequent basis.
Unsatisfactory	Performance is consistently unacceptable.

A. Performance factors (use job description as basis of this evaluation).

Administration: measures effectiveness in planning, organizing, and efficiently handling activities and eliminating unnecessary activities.	Outstanding	
	Exceeds Expectations	
	Meets Expectations	
	Below Expectations	
	Unsatisfactory	
	NA	
Knowledge of work: consider employee's skill level, knowledge and understanding of all phases of the job, and those requiring improved skills and/or experience.	Outstanding	
	Exceeds Expectations	
	Meets Expectations	
	Below Expectations	
	Unsatisfactory	
	NA	
Communication: measures effectiveness in listening to others, expressing ideas, both orally and in writing, and providing relevant and timely information to management, coworkers, subordinates, and customers.	Outstanding	
	Exceeds Expectations	
	Meets Expectations	
	Below Expectations	
	Unsatisfactory	
	NA	
Teamwork: measures how well this individual gets along with fellow employees, respects the rights of other employees, and shows a cooperative spirit.	Outstanding	
	Exceeds Expectations	
	Meets Expectations	
	Below Expectations	
	Unsatisfactory	
	NA	

Decision-making/problem-solving: measures effectiveness in understanding problems and making timely, practical decisions.	Outstanding ☐ Exceeds Expectations ☐ Meets Expectations ☐ Below Expectations ☐ Unsatisfactory ☐ NA ☐
Expense management: measures effectiveness in establishing appropriate reporting and control procedures, operating efficiently at lowest cost, staying within established budgets.	Outstanding ☐ Exceeds Expectations ☐ Meets Expectations ☐ Below Expectations ☐ Unsatisfactory ☐ NA ☐
Human resource management: measures effectiveness in selecting qualified people; evaluating subordinates' performance, strengths and development needs; providing constructive feedback; and taking appropriate and timely action with marginal or unsatisfactory performers. Also considers efforts to further the university goal of equal employment opportunity.	Outstanding ☐ Exceeds Expectations ☐ Meets Expectations ☐ Below Expectations ☐ Unsatisfactory ☐ NA ☐
Independent action: measures effectiveness in time management, initiative, and independent action within prescribed limits.	Outstanding ☐ Exceeds Expectations ☐ Meets Expectations ☐ Below Expectations ☐ Unsatisfactory ☐ NA ☐

Job knowledge: measures effectiveness in keeping knowledgeable of methods, techniques, and skills required in own job and related functions, remaining current on new developments affecting SPSU and its work activities.	Outstanding Exceeds Expectations Meets Expectations Below Expectations Unsatisfactory NA	
Leadership: measures effectiveness in accomplishing work assignments through subordinates, establishing challenging goals, delegating and coordinating effectively, promoting innovation and team effort.	Outstanding Exceeds Expectations Meets Expectations Below Expectations Unsatisfactory NA	
Managing change and improvement: measures effectiveness in initiating changes, adapting to necessary changes from old methods when they are no longer practical, identifying new methods, and generating improvement in facility's performance.	Outstanding Exceeds Expectations Meets Expectations Below Expectations Unsatisfactory NA	
Customer responsiveness: measures responsiveness and courtesy in dealing with internal staff, external customers, and vendors; employee projects a courteous manner.	Outstanding Exceeds Expectations Meets Expectations Below Expectations Unsatisfactory NA	
Personal appearance: measures neatness and personal hygiene appropriate to position.	Outstanding Exceeds Expectations Meets Expectations Below Expectations Unsatisfactory NA	

Dependability: measures how well employee complies with instructions and performs under unusual circumstances; consider record of attendance and punctuality.	Outstanding	
	Exceeds Expectations	
	Meets Expectations	
	Below Expectations	
	Unsatisfactory	
	NA	
Safety: measures individual's work habits and attitudes as they apply to working safely. Consider their contribution to accident prevention, safety awareness, ability to care for SPSU property and keep workspace safe and tidy.	Outstanding	
	Exceeds Expectations	
	Meets Expectations	
	Below Expectations	
	Unsatisfactory	
	NA	
Employee's responsiveness: measures responsiveness in completing job tasks in a timely manner.	Outstanding	
	Exceeds Expectations	
	Meets Expectations	
	Below Expectations	
	Unsatisfactory	
	NA	

B. Employee strengths and accomplishments: include those which are relevant during this evaluation period. This should be related to performance or behavioral aspects you appreciated in their performance.

C. Performance areas which need improvement:

D. Plan of action toward improved performance:

E. Employee comments:

F. Job description review section: (Please check the appropriate box.)

☐ Employee job description has been reviewed during this evaluation, and no changes have been made to the job description at this time.

☐ Employee job description has been reviewed during this evaluation, and modifications have been proposed to the job description. The modified job description is attached to this evaluation.

G. Signatures:

Employee _____ Date _____

(Signature does not necessarily denote agreement with official review and means only that the employee was given the opportunity to discuss the official review with the supervisor.)

Evaluated by _____ Date _____

Reviewed by _____ Date _____

THE SHEPHERD THEORY

Week ending: _____

Day	Regular Hours	Overtime	PTO	Total
Monday				
Tuesday				
Wednesday				
Thursday				
Friday				
Saturday				
Sunday				
Total hours				

Week ending: _____

Day	Regular Hours	Overtime	PTO	Total
Monday				
Tuesday				
Wednesday				
Thursday				
Friday				
Saturday				
Sunday				
Total hours				

_____   _____
Employee signature   Date

_____   _____
Manager signature   Date

AN ORGANIZED QUALITY SYSTEM IS A MUST-HAVE

A good quality documented quality system is also key to building integrity and increase performance in a company. The most widely accepted worldwide quality system is ISO 9001. This is an expensive journey, and smaller companies may not be able to afford to contract this. But, you cannot afford to have no written quality system. I would recommend following the ISO standards to build your quality system so, in the future, you will be set to get third party certified. Another issue would be if an ISO-certified company is going to business with you, they will need evidence that you have a quality system in place and may even ask for a copy of your quality manual. If you are interested in certification, there are many third-party underwriters that can help you with this. So I would suggest researching to find a consultant or underwriter to accomplish this certification.

Implementing ISO 9001 Quality Management System

ISO 9001-Type Quality Program

This is an outline of the requirements to build a quality system under the ISO 9001 quality system. Small companies use this as a guide to build a quality system and manual for future certification, and larger companies build a system to get certified. This can cost thousands of dollars and really needs a champion to maintain it and a dedicated management and staff, along with each employee, to have a successful program. Basically, here is the jest of this system: "say what you do," and "do what you say."

1. Context
1.1 Understand your organization and its unique context.
1.2 Clarify the needs and expectations of interested parties.
1.3 Define the scope of your quality management system.
1.4 Develop a QMS and establish documented information.
1.4.1 Establish a QMS that complies with this standard.
1.4.2 Maintain QMS documents and retain QMS records.
2. Leadership
2.1 Provide leadership by focusing on quality and customers.
2.1.1 Provide leadership by encouraging a focus on quality.
2.1.2 Provide leadership by encouraging a focus on customers.
2.2 Provide leadership by establishing a suitable quality policy.
2.2.1 Provide leadership by formulating your quality policy.
2.2.2 Provide leadership by communicating your quality policy.
2.3 Provide leadership by defining roles and responsibilities.
3. Planning
3.1 Define actions to manage risks and address opportunities.
3.1.1 Consider risks and opportunities when you plan your QMS.
3.1.2 Plan how you're going to manage risks and opportunities.
3.2 Set quality objectives and develop plans to achieve them.
3.2.1 Establish quality objectives for all relevant areas.
3.2.2 Develop plans to achieve objectives and evaluate results.
3.3 Plan changes to your quality management system.
4. Support
4.1 Support your QMS by providing the necessary resources.
4.1.1 Provide internal and external resources for your QMS.
4.1.2 Provide suitable people for your QMS and your processes.
4.1.3 Provide the infrastructure that your processes must have.
4.1.4 Provide the appropriate environment for your processes.
4.1.5 Provide monitoring, measuring, and traceability resources.
4.1.6 Provide knowledge to facilitate process operations.
4.2 Support your QMS by ensuring that people are competent.
4.3 Support your QMS by explaining how people can help.

4.4 Support your QMS by managing your communications.

4.5 Support your QMS by controlling documented information.

4.5.1 Include the documented information that your QMS needs.

4.5.2 Manage the creation and revision of documented information.

4.5.3 Control the management and use of documented information.

4.5.3.1 Control your organization's documents and records.

4.5.3.2 Control how documents and records are controlled.

5. Operations

5.1 Develop, implement, and control your operational processes.

5.2 Determine and document product and service requirements.

5.2.1 Communicate with customers and manage customer property.

5.2.2 Clarify product and service requirements and capabilities.

5.2.3 Review product and service requirements and record results.

5.2.4 Amend documents if product or service requirements change.

5.3 Establish a process to design and develop products and services.

5.3.1 create an appropriate design and development process.

5.3.2 Plan product and service design and development activities.

5.3.3 Determine product and service design and development inputs.

5.3.4 Specify how design and development process is controlled.

5.3.5 Clarify how design and development outputs are produced.

5.3.6 Review and control all design and development changes.

5.4 Monitor and control external processes, products, and services.

5.4.1 Confirm that products and services meet requirements.

5.4.2 Establish controls for external products and services.

.4.3 Discuss your requirements with external providers.

8.5 Manage and control production and service provision activities.

5.5.1 Establish controls for production and service provision.

5.5.2 Identify your outputs and control their unique identity.

5.5.3 Protect property owned by customers and external providers.

5.5.4 Preserve outputs during production and service provision.

5.5.5 Clarify and comply with all post-delivery requirements.

5.5.6 Control changes for production and service provision.

5.6 Implement arrangements to control product and service release.

5.7 Control nonconforming outputs and document actions taken.

5.7.1 Control nonconforming outputs to prevent unintended use.

5.7.2 Document nonconforming outputs and the actions taken.

6. Evaluation

6.1 Monitor, measure, analyze, and evaluate QMS.

6.1.1 Plan how to monitor, measure, analyze, and evaluate.

6.1.2 Find out how well customer expectations are being met.

6.1.3 Evaluate effectiveness, conformity, and satisfaction.

6.2 Use internal audits to examine conformance and performance.

6.2.1 Audit your quality management system at planned intervals.

6.2.2 Develop an internal audit program for your organization.

6.3 Carry out management reviews and document your results.

6.3.1 Review suitability, adequacy, effectiveness, and direction.

6.3.2 Plan and perform management reviews at planned intervals.

6.3.3 Generate management review outputs and document results.

7. Continuous Improvement

7.1 Determine improvement opportunities and make improvements.

7.2 Control nonconformities and take appropriate corrective action.

7.2.1 Correct nonconformities, causes, and consequences.

7.2.2 Document nonconformities and the actions that are taken.

7.3 Enhance the suitability, adequacy, and effectiveness of your QMS.

The Quality Pyramid

PSALM 23
(SHEPHERD'S PIE) RECIPE

1 pound of ground lamb
2 tablespoons of olive oil
1 small onion chopped fine
2 carrots chopped fine
1/2 cup of Guinness Stout
1/2 teaspoon rosemary
1/2 teaspoon of thyme
1/2 teaspoon of oregano
Salt and pepper to taste

Optional: a few squirts Frank's Hot Sauce (more or less depending on how you like it)

1 tablespoon of sugar (again more or less depending how do you like it)

Combine all ingredients and simmer without a lid until it is reduced and all the vegetables are soft and the meat has been browned.

The mash:

5 medium-sized russet potatoes boiled in water with 1 teaspoon of salt
1/2 cup of sour cream
1/4–1/2 cup of milk depends on how thick you like your potatoes
1/2 stick of butter or margarine
1 tablespoon of dried or fresh chives

Boil the potatoes until Soft, and then mash them using all of the ingredients above.

The assembly:

In a casserole dish, put in the meat sauce, The next layer is one box of frozen peas. The final layer is the mashed potatoes; and on top of the mashed potatoes, sprinkle cheddar cheese, pepper, and parsley. Put in a 325° F oven for one hour. Then let it set 10 minutes prior to serving. This allows it to stabilize. Enjoy!

ABOUT THE AUTHOR

Mark E. Peters is an electrical engineer and has held various position in his twenty-seven years in the corporate world. He started his career as a systems project engineer. After a few years of project work, he was transferred to another division to manage a controls division company with approximately fifty employees. Then he was moved to director of engineering and oversaw one company and four engineering departments. After twenty-five years with one company, he was hired away to another company that brought him on as a VP of engineering. After three years and eight new products, along with multiple patents, he left the corporate world to start his own controls company with an Italian partner. After twelve years of growth and going from four employees to fifteen and nearly fifty worldwide, Mark and his partner sold the company and restarted a new cutting-edge wireless company. Today Mark is now retired doing consulting and enjoying his hobbies of playing guitar, reading, writing, photography, and cooking.

CPSIA information can be obtained
at www.ICGtesting.com
Printed in the USA
FSHW010251240421
80665FS